A Defence of Nihilism

This book offers a philosophical defence of nihilism. The authors argue that the concept of nihilism has been employed pejoratively by almost all philosophers and religious leaders to indicate a widespread cultural crisis of truth, meaning, or morals. Many religious believers think atheism leads to moral chaos (because it leads to nihilism), and atheists typically insist that we can make life meaningful through our own actions (thereby avoiding nihilism). In this way, both sides conflate the cosmic sense of meaning at stake with a social sense of meaning. This book charts a third course between extremist and alarmist views of nihilism. It casts doubt on the assumption that nihilism is something to fear, or a problem which human culture should overcome by way of seeking, discovering, or making meaning. In this way, the authors believe that a revised understanding of nihilism can help remove a significant barrier of misunderstanding between religious believers and atheists. *A Defence of Nihilism* will be of interest to scholars and students in philosophy, religion, and other disciplines who are interested in questions surrounding the meaning of life.

James Tartaglia is Professor of Metaphysical Philosophy at Keele University, UK. He is author of *Philosophy in a Meaningless Life* (2016) and *Philosophy in a Technological World: Gods and Titans* (2020).

Tracy Llanera is Assistant Research Professor of Philosophy at the University of Connecticut and faculty affiliate at the UConn Asian and Asian American Studies Institute. She is author of *Richard Rorty: Outgrowing Modern Nihilism* (2020).

Routledge Focus on Philosophy

Routledge Focus on Philosophy is an exciting and innovative new series, capturing and disseminating some of the best and most exciting new research in philosophy in short book form. Peer reviewed and at a maximum of fifty thousand words shorter than the typical research monograph, *Routledge Focus on Philosophy* titles are available in both ebook and print on demand format. Tackling big topics in a digestible format the series opens up important philosophical research for a wider audience, and as such is invaluable reading for the scholar, researcher and student seeking to keep their finger on the pulse of the discipline. The series also reflects the growing interdisciplinarity within philosophy and will be of interest to those in related disciplines across the humanities and social sciences.

Confucianism and the Philosophy of Well-Being
Richard Kim

Neurofunctional Prudence and Morality
A Philosophical Theory
Marcus Arvan

The Epistemology and Morality of Human Kinds
Marion Godman

A Defence of Nihilism
James Tartaglia and Tracy Llanera

For more information about this series, please visit: www.routledge.com/Routledge-Focus-on-Philosophy/book-series/RFP

A Defence of Nihilism

James Tartaglia and Tracy Llanera

NEW YORK AND LONDON

First published 2021
by Routledge
52 Vanderbilt Avenue, New York, NY 10017

and by Routledge
2 Park Square, Milton Park, Abingdon, Oxon, OX14 4RN

Routledge is an imprint of the Taylor & Francis Group, an informa business

© 2021 Taylor & Francis

The right of James Tartaglia and Tracy Llanera to be identified as authors of this work has been asserted by them in accordance with sections 77 and 78 of the Copyright, Designs and Patents Act 1988.

All rights reserved. No part of this book may be reprinted or reproduced or utilised in any form or by any electronic, mechanical, or other means, now known or hereafter invented, including photocopying and recording, or in any information storage or retrieval system, without permission in writing from the publishers.

Trademark notice: Product or corporate names may be trademarks or registered trademarks, and are used only for identification and explanation without intent to infringe.

Library of Congress Cataloging-in-Publication Data
Names: Tartaglia, James, 1973– author. | Llanera, Tracy, author.
Title: A defence of nihilism / James Tartaglia and Tracy Llanera.
Description: New York : Routledge, 2021. | Includes bibliographical references and index.
Identifiers: LCCN 2020037181 (print) | LCCN 2020037182 (ebook) | ISBN 9780367230166 (hardback) | ISBN 9780429277962 (ebook)
Subjects: LCSH: Nihilism (Philosophy)
Classification: LCC B828.3 .T37 2021 (print) | LCC B828.3 (ebook) | DDC 149/.8—dc23
LC record available at https://lccn.loc.gov/2020037181
LC ebook record available at https://lccn.loc.gov/2020037182

ISBN: 978-0-367-23016-6 (hbk)
ISBN: 978-0-429-27796-2 (ebk)

Typeset in Times New Roman
by codeMantra

For Charlie (a dog), Slifer, and Obelisk (snakes)

Contents

Acknowledgements ix

1 Much Ado about Nothing 1
2 A Brief History of Nihilism 13
3 Nil Desperandum 27
4 Nihil Sine Deo 39
5 Revaluating Nihilism 53

Index 61

Acknowledgements

This project began at Keele University, where I (Tracy) was a School of Politics, Philosophy, International Relations and Environment (SPIRE) Research Fellow in Spring 2018. James was my academic sponsor. I was pretty much sick throughout my stay (it was my first experience of winter in the Northern Hemisphere) so I'm relieved that something good came out of all that coughing.

I am grateful to the Keele philosophers for their warm welcome. I thank Heather Battaly and Michael Lynch for inviting Routledge to the University of Connecticut Humanities Institute in Fall 2018. Pitching a project in person, I found out then, was much more fun and rewarding ('it's a book about nothing!').

We thank Andrew Weckenmann, our editor, and Allie Simmons, editorial assistant, for their support from start to finish. We are also grateful to the anonymous reviewers for their feedback.

1 Much Ado about Nothing

There might be a masterplan for the human race, set in place by the creator, or the creators. Meaning may be built into the fabric of reality, whether reality was created or not, and this may have implications for what we should be doing with ourselves. The final goal, the one which makes our strivings and sufferings either worthwhile or wasted, may be a preordained destiny, or it may be a target we could hit or miss. Perhaps we have made good progress towards it, or perhaps our choices have led us astray; it's hard to know without knowing what the goal is, which is something the human race has never been able to agree about.

But put all those ideas on hold for a moment and just suppose there is nothing of cosmic significance going on at all. We are just people going in and out of rooms, sending electronic messages, falling in love, eating apples, signing nuclear non-proliferation treaties, and so on. All these things go on, some of them are really important to us, but they don't add up to anything in the cosmic scheme of things, for the simple reason that *there isn't a cosmic scheme of things*. Suppose the great science-fiction writer H.G. Wells was wrong when he said that, 'The world has a greater purpose than happiness; our lives are to serve God's purpose, and that purpose aims not at man as an end, but works through him to greater issues'.[1] Suppose there is no purpose for us, not even happiness. What you are being asked to suppose is the truth of nihilism.

Or at least, that's one interpretation of what 'nihilism' means. The word literally means 'nothing-ism' and is currently a strong contender for the most ambiguous word in philosophy, a true nothing-word. Some think this is par for the course. At the back of philosopher Nolen Gertz's recent book on nihilism, for instance, there is a glossary of terms providing one-sentence explanations of existentialism, metaphysics, and postmodernism, but when it comes to nihilism, he draws the line. For that entry, we are told only that nihilism is wanting 'complicated ideas reduced to one sentence made easily available in the back of a book'.[2] Back in 1950, philosopher and novelist Ernst Jünger said that, 'A good definition of nihilism would be the equivalent of revealing the cause of cancer' – because he thought nihilism was the elusive thought-disease which produced the Nazis.[3] Michael Gillespie, who has been very influential in forging contemporary understandings of nihilism, ultimately concludes that it is a kind of experience, in which we look out at the void of meaning in which our reality exists and become lost for words. But as Gillespie and others have noted, the lack of clarity around the word 'nihilism' puts it in danger of becoming a catch-all for everything bad. Without clarity, it becomes a shape-shifting obstacle to a rational debate.[4]

Some philosophers do use the word perfectly clearly, but in special senses that draw on its literal meaning. So there is 'mereological nihilism', according to which there are no ordinary objects, such as chairs, only particles arranged in a way that produces chair-experiences, and there is also 'metaphysical nihilism', the view that there might have been no objects at all. But all that is far removed from the mainstream discussion of nihilism, in which it is usually something bad, although what exactly is never pinned down. We think the best way to use the word is for the claim that human life is meaningless, in the cosmic sense of there being no overall plan for our existence. This is the dominant meaning history has given it, to which the other ideas circulating around it can be easily related and illuminated. It's a very short history too. Unlike 'nice', which Shakespeare used to mean fussy, lustful, detailed, and trivial, it hasn't had long to shape-shift, its clientele have been tiny in comparison, and it was introduced for a specific purpose. But we will leave the history until the next chapter.

If you believe that 'nihilism' (in our simple sense) is true, then what follows? Something very terrible indeed, it is widely supposed. Nihilism is regarded as a subversive and dangerous doctrine. According to the *Internet Encyclopedia of Philosophy*, 'A true nihilist would believe in nothing, have no loyalties, and no purpose other than, perhaps, a will to destroy'.[5] In popular culture, the nihilist is bad to the bone. The Joker, in the iconic Heath Ledger portrayal, doesn't care about money or infamy – he's much too bad for that, he doesn't care about anything at all. He just wants to cause chaos – if 'wants' is the right word, for perhaps it's better to describe him as a chaotic, destructive force of nature. He's as bad as you can get because he's a nihilist through and through, the ultimate threat – a criminal you can't reason with because he doesn't want anything. You can't empathise with his perspective to talk some sense into him, because that would suck you into the abyss of nihilism which has already done for that poor soul.

Now how is that supposed to follow from the view that there's no meaning of life? We mean 'follow' in the ordinary sense of, 'ah, it's raining – that's why he took the umbrella – it follows'. How is believing that life has no cosmic significance supposed to turn you into the Joker, or, more mundanely, one of those people in the dark corners of the internet who despise everything about life and are eager to tell you about it. Ordinary folk aren't nihilists, it is thought, that's only for life-hating and angry people, or perhaps for people in utter despair. Or in another sense the word is sometimes given, perhaps ordinary folk are actually the worse culprits, because nihilism is an unthinking immersion in trivia which results when you don't care about the important things in life, or they've ceased to be important to you. In this chapter, we'll focus on the more popular destructive/self-destructive senses (we'll see how the 'trivia' idea became involved in the history chapter). Since our aim is to persuade you of the attractions of nihilism, the first step is to understand why hate, subversion, or despair have been thought to follow from nihilism, and why they don't.

The crucial reasoning which has given nihilism a bad name, we suggest, is as follows. If you don't think there's a meaning of life, then you see that absolutely everything about the way we live is based on a false premise. We have standards of moral behaviour – you shouldn't cheat or hurt people for personal advantage or sordid satisfaction, you should play by the rules which make things fair and pleasant for everyone. And with those standards in place, we strive to achieve all kinds of goals, ranging from making friends at school or buying your first house to winning Olympic gold or unifying quantum mechanics with relativity theory. But that only makes sense if there's a meaning of life (or so the reasoning goes). If there isn't, then it's all pointless anyway. It doesn't matter if we turn our meaningless existence into a living hell. When the 'nihilist' realises this, they look out at a world of public institutions upholding illusory moral codes, and people earnestly pursuing pointless goals, and their natural response is contempt. These fools haven't realised that life is meaningless! They haven't realised they're wasting their time! When they observe life going on, it's like watching a drug addict desperately digging in the ground to find the stash they buried, when you know it's not there because you already dug it up and flushed it down the toilet. You despise their goal and know they won't achieve it, but they hope to achieve it and desperately want to, so you feel contempt for them.

Once the 'nihilist' has reached the contempt stage, the question of where to go next is something of a moot point; different ideas about what nihilism entails, often conflated with what it amounts to, spin off at this point. Perhaps the nihilist will get destructive. They need to do something about the contemptible world they live in, so they try to disrupt it, or just disillusion everyone else in light of the nihilist truth. But the problem with taking this stance is that it must mean the nihilist has goals of their own: they want to destroy and disrupt. Why should they care? Caring undermines the reason they want to destroy, namely that people care about things but shouldn't. Perhaps they just can't tolerate the ignorance they see around them, in which case destructive nihilism emerges as a surprisingly high-brow and moralistic stance, one which shows deep concern for others to live in tune with the truth. But given what the truth in question amounts to, that makes no sense. A world of chaos in which you have to sleep with a gun under your pillow would be no more or less meaningless than our own. The sleepy businessman mindlessly trotting down to the office is being just as true to nihilism as the Joker. The businessman doesn't know, we may suppose. But once we tell him, he may still decide to carry on as usual; if nothing matters, why not?

Proactive nihilism of this kind doesn't follow from the contempt stage, then. There's no parallel between 'he took his umbrella because it's raining' and 'she's trying to cause chaos because she's realised the truth of nihilism'. If the contempt unleashes your destructive passion, that's just because of what you're like. Others might laugh with derision, feel their contempt mellow into pity, or not care enough to give it another thought.

So what about a more passive response? That seems more promising, because if nothing matters, realising this shouldn't inspire you to action. Let's suppose the nihilist simply feels their hopes and fears for life fade away. None of their old goals seem worth investing any effort into anymore. Since they've lost interest in everything that used to get them out of bed in the morning, should they commit suicide? That would show they care whether they live or die, and they're not supposed to care about anything. The 19th-century German philosopher, Schopenhauer, made a similar objection to suicide: that it gives in to the passion you want to avoid.[6] But that neglects the practicalities of the passive nihilist's situation, for if they're capable of one more pointless act of will, it will at least be their last. If they live, they have to continue observing the contemptuous human non-drama. And they will feel self-contempt too, because of the goals their biology forces on them – they will genuinely want to eat, for example. So although not entirely consistent, suicide is probably their best option – assuming that nihilism doesn't simply paralyse them, in which case they're doomed to die of dehydration. It seems that realising life is meaningless is not just dangerous, but positively deadly. What follows from the contempt stage is death.

If nihilism leads directly to doom, then you can see how it picked up its bad reputation. But doesn't it strike you as bizarre to suppose that doom might follow from absence of cosmic meaning? That sounds like something a religious fundamentalist might say: turn away from God's meaning and you will face only doom and despair. You'd expect most people to disagree with that, especially atheists. So let's look once again at how we got to the contempt stage.

The reasoning is that since our goals and morals are premised on there being a meaning of life, then if there isn't one, we're all wasting our time. But goals and morals needn't be premised on a meaning of life *for nihilists*. We can have mundane reasons for pursuing our goals and trying to be nice. We can go shopping so there'll be something in the fridge to cook for dinner, and the thought that this doesn't contribute to a cosmic plan needn't concern us in the least. The meaninglessness of life needn't make us feel it was a wasted effort, if the dinner tells us it wasn't. The reason we don't go around destroying things can just be that we feel for others and don't want to be arrested. You could ramp it up to an almost cosmic level by saying that the ultimate motivation is pleasure, or satisfaction, or the alleviation of boredom and suffering. But then, you end up saying something so fuzzy that it can fuzzily apply to all the billions of reasons we have for doing things, like texting or brushing our teeth. Some of us nihilists just can't see the point, because we don't think there's a meaning of life and feel no need for a substitute like 'happiness' to make up for it. We do different things for different reasons.

Maybe you think this is too quick: if everything is pointless, how can individual activities, which are part of that 'everything', still have a point? Well, look at it like this. Suppose there are 360 people, each heading in a different direction corresponding to the 360 degrees on a compass; one is heading due North, another due South, etc. The group of all 360 people isn't heading in any particular direction, since the individuals are all heading in different directions. But the fact that the group isn't heading in a particular direction obviously doesn't mean the individuals aren't. As a matter of fact, they are. Likewise, if there's no meaning to human existence as a whole, that doesn't mean there isn't any meaning in individual human lives. As a matter of fact, there is. We project meaning onto our lives by wanting to do things, and by finding things important, boring, outrageous, unjust, beautiful, or whatever. Nihilists can regard that as the real thing, the only meaning there is for us, although other animals must have their meanings too – when a wolf is expelled from the pack, that must mean something to it. If this kind of everyday meaning required ultimate purpose, then the truth of nihilism would be strictly impossible, and whatever it is, it isn't that. There's no contradiction involved in supposing that our reality lacks cosmic meaning.

Do believers feel motivation only because they believe in ultimate purpose? Some, possibly, but if any have actually achieved this feat, then it can't have been many, given that believers text and brush their teeth too. The much more sensible and believable view is that the meaning of life provides the most important motivation for our lives as a whole, and that if we live good lives in accordance with our religion, then maybe, in some small way, we contribute to God's plan. That represents a big disagreement with the nihilist, but not an impenetrable barrier. Both can accept mundane reasons for doing things – reasons you might be really passionate about and goals you might pour all your effort into. It's just that the nihilist stops there, while the believer thinks that there's something more important. The believer thinks that the nihilist is missing out and the nihilist is at liberty to disagree.

A personal anecdote may help here. One of us (James) was once in a jazz-funk band that played at Christian music festivals, doing Herbie Hancock covers and the like; most of the musicians were Christians, and the leader was thinking of going into the priesthood. At one of these festivals, the conversation turned to religion, unsurprisingly, and James cautiously suggested that being an atheist can't be that bad, pretty much the same really. 'You can live', the bandleader replied, with genuine but light-hearted disparagement. It was a good answer. You can live, and that's all the atheist thinks there is to do, while the believer thinks that the atheist has turned their back on the divine plan, the most important thing of all. There's plenty of room for toleration here, because when it comes to life, we're all in the same boat. The book of Ecclesiastes in the Bible is a clear statement of nihilism about mortal life, which it calls 'vanity of vanities'. 'All is vanity!' it declares, for in pursuit of our mundane goals, we're in 'pursuit of wind'. The final conclusion is not nihilism, of course, for mortal life is being contrasted with the afterlife and God's plan. But for the nihilist, the eternal significance of an extra something they don't believe in needn't cast life in a negative light. They can like pursuing wind – and believers evidently can too, they just don't think that's all they're doing. Militant atheists, like the religious fundamentalists who inspire their intolerance, show little interest in this common ground, but rather focus on differences in their efforts to convert. Maybe that's because they're not nihilists, but rather believers in a secular meaning of life.

Only an extremist could think that brushing your teeth is motivated by the meaning of life, and that if nihilism were true, we wouldn't be able to do it. And yet, it is a variant of this extreme view which makes nihilism seem dangerous. The variant is that we need to *believe* in a meaning of life to feel motivation. When the passive nihilist realises there's no such meaning, the rest of the world doesn't grind to a halt, only they do. Yet if we can be motivated to do things without that belief, there's no reason for the nihilist to do anything they wouldn't have done anyway.

Two major intellectual pressures lie in the background of the kind of confused thinking about nihilism we've been exposing. The first is religious teaching that the meaning of life is all that really matters. The second is the highly influential 19th-century German philosopher, Nietzsche, whose interpretation of that religious teaching made it seem relevant to atheists. He thought centuries of religious indoctrination had led people to invest all value and significance in an imaginary meaning of life somewhere beyond the clouds, making things in real life seem as if they're only worthwhile because of it. So when the brainwashing subsided, and the masses lost their faith, they'd find themselves confined to the real world which they'd already stripped of meaning, and where the 'all is vanity' of Ecclesiastes would now become the total 'all' of nihilism. This presented an opportunity for Nietzsche's aggressively anti-religious agenda, because then a better class of people could arise, guided by his teachings, to invest life with a meaning supposedly un-poisoned by life-hating religion.

It's a captivating story, but not very realistic. Christians pray to be 'delivered from temptation' – from the pleasures of the flesh, for instance, which is something Saint Augustine struggled particularly hard with – so the idea that even the most devout Christians manage to transfer all their passion to another world is pie in the sky.

At most, this is an ideal, something you try your best to achieve, *if* you interpret your religion that way. Nihilism might be a paralysing prospect for someone who achieved this, but such a person is the least likely to lose their faith. Ordinary people who lose their faith frequently manage to get over it and carry on. So why born-and-bred atheists would have a problem with nihilism beats us. Nietzsche was born in 1844, the son of a Lutheran pastor. Atheism was bound to seem of great personal and social significance to him, and his characteristically exuberant response was to accord it, and himself, the highest possible world-historical significance.

Now nihilism is not strictly speaking a consequence of atheism, because if all of the world's religions have it completely wrong, human life might still be meaningful. Meaning might be built into the fabric of reality without there being any builder. This is not unfathomable, since we are all familiar with inherently meaningful realities in the shape of thoughts: if you're thinking about Paris, the meaning of Paris is built into the nature of your thought. Reality might be one big thought, or something like that, but it's a weird idea and we're not recommending it. So let's just say that nihilism *basically* follows from atheism, in that given the kind of things most atheists believe about the nature of reality, they ought to embrace it.

The problem is they don't. We live in a world of non-believers trying to make their lives meaningful and believing that the meaning of life is love, peace, happiness, knowledge, or power. It's usually innocent enough, but not always, such as if you think fame gives you a meaningful life – fame for doing anything, no matter how bad. Secular meanings have a disadvantage to religious ones in that they needn't even be supposed to be morally good, while the religious ones have the disadvantage of tending to promote moral inflexibility. Nevertheless, most people get along just fine with their personal beliefs in a meaning of life, secular or religious. The secular ones become more concerning, however, when they leave the personal sphere to try to emulate the religious ones more exactly, becoming beliefs in a destiny of mankind. This can take the form of a worldwide communist revolution, the perfecting of our species through eugenics, our supposedly inevitable future of merging with technology, or our need to create superior artificial intelligences to replace us. When science and politics get hold of the meaning of life in a secular context, it's at least as scary as the Spanish Inquisition.

Accepting nihilism is having a negative belief: you *don't* believe in a meaning of life. But not believing can be positive if the belief in question drives outcomes most of us have not chosen and do not want. It's positive when belief in an ultimate goal is thought to justify untold quantities of sacrifice, disruption, and risk along the way to it. Nihilists don't believe in a meaning of life, so they don't think we're destined to create paradise on earth. Things could go completely wrong – we could make ourselves extinct, as almost happened in the Cuban Missile Crisis. Things could take a very bad turn for the worse, as happened in the Second World War. Nihilism removes the justification for thinking that everything is bound to turn out fine in the end. Far from being the disease it is often portrayed as, then, nihilism is a remedy for atheists. It fosters a healthy scepticism about big plans, especially when they concern the human race as a whole. Big plans can be great, but they're justified by the reasoning behind them and the popular mandate they receive, not the meaning of life. The bigger they come, the more reasoning and mandate they require, and your hunch about our inevitable destiny is not good enough, no good at all.

That's not all that nihilism has to recommend it, however, for it is a philosophical view. To describe yourself as a nihilist is to declare your lack of patience with the woeful scientistic positivism that tells us we aren't allowed to ask questions unless our answers can be tested in a laboratory. That kind of attitude is well past its sell-by-date, for as has been realised for the best part of a century now, it completely undermines itself – it rests on the view that only statements that can be scientifically tested are significant ... which itself isn't a view that can be scientifically tested. All kinds of questions are worth asking, and the nihilist sees no problem in asking the same question of the meaning of life as religious believers, just giving a different, equally unverifiable answer – and none the worse for that. This process was as philosophically enlightening as for the religious believer, because now the nihilist can see their life in a cosmic perspective: an all-encompassing, meaningless one. You might call it a spiritual vision, but it's really just a philosophical one. It's something you might overlook your whole life, just never notice, and it brings a greater self-awareness with clear benefits.

Religion and atheism need to make up, and if atheists can stop feeling queasy about nihilism, it could really help. We all need to live together and neither side is going away. Religions have embarked on the project of conversation throughout history, and with the advent of intolerant atheists, this is now very much a two-way process. But taking an aggressive, colonising attitude shows a lack of self-confidence which both sides need to grow out of. If life with religion is so much better, or more important, then religion will spread and atheism is not a threat. Similarly, if the arguments for atheism are good, or more accurately, if the arguments for religious belief are no good, then those open to rational persuasion will come around of their own accord. Both sides need to stop seeing the other as a threat and blaming all the ills of the world on them. Many crimes have been perpetrated in the name of religion, but with the advent of atheist totalitarian regimes in the 20th century, we've seen that both sides can be just as bad.

A positive development would be for atheists to take the next step to nihilism – the philosophical step. Both sides would then enter the same cosmic conceptual space, where dialogue becomes possible. And although calling yourself an 'atheist' may be factually correct, it defines you in opposition to religion. It is the desire to avoid this, among other things, which motivates the alternative terminology of 'humanism'. But that strikes us as a bit wishy-washy ('tigerism' isn't an option, we take it?). And it's too human-centric, in a world where we've just started learning to care more about the environment. Although not what's intended, a big game hunter might justify his treating animals as of no more significance than sport for humans in terms of his 'humanism' – the word would fit nicely. But the main problem with 'humanism' is that it sounds like a secular substitute for religion, which for many is what it has become. And if it's going to be a proper substitute, it needs a meaning of life: one people make for themselves. But we can't make a meaning of life. Even if a popularly mandated goal for humanity were to arise one day in the distant future, it still wouldn't be what we're here for, it'd just be what we'd all decided we want to do – and we might fail.

Nihilists enter the same conceptual space as the religious, seeing no reason to miss out, but they most certainly do not allow religious beliefs to frame their own, for then their nihilism would be a choice to ignore the best thing about life, or even to seal their own doom – so nobody in their right mind would opt for nihilism in a religious context. It's defined by the absence of a meaning of life, which is an idea that arose with religion, but which atheists have shown themselves very partial to as well, with plans devised ever since the 18th-century Enlightenment for building heaven on earth. Nihilists believe neither in a meaning of life imposed by God nor in one supposedly made by humans. Nihilism spans divides in a conciliatory and illuminating way.

Now you might think 'nihilism' is an odd choice for a word to try to rehabilitate, since it has already been claimed by two sets of proud owners: the amoralists, misanthropes and anarchists, and the 'culture critics' who use it to disparage modern life. It indicates belief in nothing where others believe in something; the first group don't believe in morality, people, or law, while the second think that our trivial contemporary lives reveal a lack of proper purpose. But just as these ideas belong to the vague *status quo* of current usage, so does the idea that nihilism is a philosophical doctrine connected with the meaning of life – otherwise, you wouldn't have bought this book and read this far, we'd wager. And while it's true that 'nihilism' has had a negative connotation for most (not all) of its history, that's only because it was viewed in a religious context. So if the connotation isn't justified, we shouldn't allow the confusion to live on. It encourages both believers and atheists to carry on fearing nihilism and acting accordingly. Until the word is reclaimed, its very existence encourages belief in a meaning of life. People who are positive about not believing in a meaning of life will hardly want the word used in a way that means: the terrible consequences of not believing in a meaning of life. Other people's misunderstandings should not force us to invent a new word.

Do nihilists not believe in anything? The 'in' is crucial, since they can obviously believe lots of things. Well, in an innocent sense, they can indeed believe *in* things. They might believe in the fire brigade when their house is burning down, since they trust the firefighters will do everything they can. Or they might believe in their friend during a difficult period, since they believe he or she will have the strength to get through it. But nihilists do not believe in a destiny guiding us, or in the power of the human race to overcome all obstacles. If you are a nihilist, you might believe in people to the extent that you think that, probably, most of them are basically OK, and hope the ones you struggle to get along with would classify you that way too. But having seen through the most influential attempts to give overall significance and destiny to the human race, namely religious meanings of life, nihilists ought to be very wary when they encounter others. Succumb, and you may find yourself seeing us as out-of-control bacteria spreading havoc across our planet, because you have seen our true biological meaning. Or you may see us as an intelligence set to shed its biological form to emanate around the universe, because you have seen our true informational meaning. Or you may see us as a manifestation of free-market forces working their way through history as a replacement for Darwinian natural selection, because you have seen our true economic meaning.[7] That's the danger nihilism helps us avoid: the danger of allowing a non-moral substitute for the meaning of life to develop.

Notes

1. Wells, *Anticipations*, 340–3.
2. Gertz, *Nihilism*, 188 (this was perhaps intended as a protest against the demand for a glossary by Gertz's publishers).
3. Jünger is cited in Goudsblom, *Nihilism and Culture*, 15.
4. Gillespie, 'Nihilism after Nietzsche', 80–100.
5. Pratt, 'Nihilism'.
6. Schopenhauer, *The World as Will and Representation, Vol. 1* (1818), 398ff.
7. For contemporary advocates of these three ideas, see Gray's *Straw Dogs*, Kurzweil's *The Singularity Is Near* and Ridley's *The Evolution of Everything*.

Bibliography

Gertz, Nolen. *Nihilism*. Cambridge, MA: The MIT Press, 2019.
Gillespie, Michael Allen. 'Nihilism after Nietzsche'. *Bollettino*
Goudsblom, Johan. *Nihilism and Culture*. Oxford: Basil Blackwell, 1980.
Gray, John. *Straw Dogs*. London: Granta Books, 2002.
Kurzweil, Ray. *The Singularity Is Near*. New York: Penguin, 2005.
Pratt, Alan. 'Nihilism'. *Internet Encyclopedia of Philosophy*. Accessed June 20, 2020. https://www.iep.utm.edu/nihilism/
Ridley, Matt. *The Evolution of Everything*. London: Fourth Estate, 2015.
Schopenhauer, Arthur. *The World as Will and Representation, Vols. 1 and 2*. Translated by E.F.J. Payne. New York: Dover Publications, 1966.
Wells, H.G. *Anticipations of the Reaction of Mechanical and Scientific Progress upon Human Life and Thought*. London: Chapman and Hall, 1901.

2 A Brief History of Nihilism

Discussions of 'nihil' abound throughout the history of Christian philosophy and theology. It was one of the great obsessions of Saint Augustine (354–30), who thought the continual activity of God was needed to prevent reality from collapsing into nothingness. In the 12th century, the Catholic Church twice condemned as heretical a doctrine called 'nihilianism'. This held that Jesus, considered as a man, was nothing – in the sense that he was never essentially a man and was always divine. 'Nihilism', however, was born in 18th-century Germany, along with its twin, 'the meaning of life'.

'Nihilism' was first coined by Friedrich Lebrecht Götze, a deacon in the church at Zwickau, Saxony, in his ambitious and lengthy book called *De Nonismo et Nihilismo in Theologia* (1733). Discussion of 'nihilism' started to catch on about 50 years later. Nobody knows if it was adopted from Götze or re-invented, but those developments happened just down the road among people who read widely. He wrote in Latin, under the Latinised name Goetzius, and in the preface he claims two new words as his inventions: nonismo (not-ism) and nihilismo (nothing-ism). Götze's original project was to view the world through the lens of nothingness and he provides a compendium of writings about not-this, not-that, nothing, and nobody. The word 'theologia' in the title is a bit misleading, since although there's plenty about theological topics, such as God creating the world from nothing, Götze's sources include modern philosophers like Hobbes and Spinoza, popular literature such as *Robinson Crusoe*, and the pioneering French journalist Anne-Marguerite Petit du Noyer, whose prose-poem, 'Tout, ou Rien' (All, or Nothing), Götze reproduces – here's a flavour of it:

> [T]here is NOTHING in the world but what tends to advance the designs of a certain kind of man, who will stop at NOTH-ING, despite the injustices, to show the whole world that he is

persuaded there is NOTHING at all in Virtue, in Morality, or in Religion, and that NOTHING will stop him from overturning everything.[1]

Götze only gave us the word, as we're reminded by the contemporary nihilistic resonance of Madam du Noyer's poem. The idea of supposing nothing where others assume something is as old as the hills – and Götze was right that it can be illuminating. Which particular 'nothing' his word was to gravitate towards was yet to be determined, however.

That happened in its next appearance, where Nihilism is a person talking to us. It is one of four unlikely characters, together with Metaphysics, Humanity, and Eternity, in a 1787 book by Jakob Hermann Obereit. Obereit was a doctor by trade, with a penchant for the mystical and occult, and he spent his life travelling around Germany mingling with the leading intellectuals of the day. The basic plot of his book is that Humanity relies on Metaphysics, but Nihilism drives Metaphysics to desperation, so Humanity turns to Eternity to save the day. But to make any sense of that, we need to backtrack into the context.

Europe had been blighted by religious wars in the previous century and the German people had taken the brunt of it. In the Thirty Years War (1618–48), some 20% of the German population are thought to have perished, and the French emerged as the dominant cultural and political force in the region. Religion had been given a bad name, the Germans felt aggrieved, and the French were starting to have some worryingly radical ideas, which were about to explode, a couple of years after Obereit published his book, into the French Revolution.

The French Enlightenment prioritised reason and science over faith and tradition, and its 18th-century 'philosophes', such as Voltaire and Rousseau, dreamt of perfecting human life with human ingenuity; of building a paradise in harmony with the benevolent natural order, rather than waiting for God's paradise. Some were 'materialists', a new label that arose at this time for advocates of the ancient metaphysical theory of atomism, which holds that everything that exists is built from the smallest possible atom-bricks. Atomism had been associated with opposition to religious institutions since ancient times. Greek philosopher Epicurus, and his Roman follower Lucretius, held that there's no point wasting your time worshipping gods, since they don't bother themselves with us insignificant humans. Some of the materialists they now inspired, such as Baron d'Holbach, born in Germany but resident in Paris, dared to go beyond the old view of divine indifference to openly endorse out-and-out atheism. Holbach held that humans are part of a godless, atomistic nature, and that religion was an obstacle to it running its naturally benevolent course – one that needed to be removed.

You'd be hard-pressed to identify an atheist in the ancient world – even Theodorus 'the Atheist' (c. 340–250 B.C.) probably wasn't, and while the Indian Charvaka school (7th century B.C. onwards) is a distinct possibility, with its opposition to the priesthood and promotion of pleasure-seeking, we mainly know about it from later writers telling us how very wrong it all was. The medieval period was holier than ever, and even when you get to modern times, Thomas Hobbes (1588–1679), the English materialist most notorious for suspected atheism, was still only suspected. All that changed with the French Enlightenment. Atheism now showed its face, and although rarely as boldly as with Holbach, there arose great suspicion of new philosophical accounts of the nature of reality (i.e. metaphysics) which might somehow imply atheism, unwittingly or otherwise. The deeper worry was that reason and argument might not lead us to God, whose divine order justified the authority of church and state. Major developments were taking place in German metaphysical philosophy in the late 18th century, and the suspicion they were held in is the context in which 'nihilism' first became a topic of conversation.

Obereit's book, in which Nihilism is a leading character, followed in the wake of an acrimonious dispute between one of the main representatives of Germany's Enlightenment movement, the Jewish philosopher Moses Mendelssohn, and F.H. Jacobi, a pivotal figure in the history of nihilism. 'Old Fritz', as Jacobi would become known, represented the traditional religious old-guard: he opposed the Enlightenment, he opposed Romanticism too (more on that later), and he was one of the earliest critics of the French Revolution. He saw atheism and chaos rising all around him and he fought back with his pen. He was also a critic of the philosophy of Immanuel Kant, by far the most important development in German (or any) philosophy in the 1780s. It was Kant's philosophy that inspired Obereit's contribution to the discussions that Jacobi and Mendelssohn's dispute sparked off.

The dispute occurred because Jacobi claimed that Mendelssohn's lifelong friend, the playwright G.E. Lessing, had told him, shortly before he died, that he was a 'Spinozist'. This was a reference to the great Jewish philosopher of the 17th century, Baruch Spinoza, who held that there's only one substantial reality: God. Weirdly enough, this maximally religious-sounding view inspired charges of materialism and atheism, because Spinoza's belief that his all-encompassing God-substance could be understood in terms of material nature (as well as in other ways) sounded too much like materialism. For Jacobi to accuse Lessing of being a Spinozist, then, was considered tantamount to saying that he was a materialist, and since the bridge between materialism and atheism had been crossed, an atheist.

Jacobi and Mendelssohn exchanged heated letters about this, with Mendelssohn trying to distance his deceased friend from Spinoza's actual views, while nevertheless finding a reasonable core to the latter. Then, Jacobi published the correspondence without permission. Feeling betrayed, Mendelssohn was in such a hurry to make a public response that he headed off to the publishers in the bitter cold without his coat – he fell ill, died four days later, and his friends blamed Old Fritz. J.G. Hamann, another prominent opponent of the Enlightenment, wrote to Jacobi to say that, 'Certainly you are to be blamed and this is your unacknowledged guilt, that you have sought and presupposed *truth* in a Jew, a natural enemy of it'.[2] Although this kind of blatant anti-Semitism existed on the Enlightenment side of the argument too (e.g. Holbach), it does make you wonder to what extent opposition to Mendelssohn and Spinoza was based on reasoned argument.

The dispute made Jacobi famous and Spinoza's philosophy a hot topic. It rolled on for years, because the underlying issues were reason vs. faith and innovation vs. tradition, and the stakes looked high in a changing and tumultuous world. Perhaps a free-thinking reliance on reason would lead us to Spinozism and atheism, as Jacobi was suggesting, and so contribute to undermining the traditional political and moral order, with chaos being the result. This kind of concern was later developed into its most dramatic form by the infamous Joseph de Maistre, who argued that if stability and peace were the aim, then the last thing we needed was reason, which just leads to endless bickering, and change after disputed-change. Maistre saw no benevolent nature for reason to bring us into harmony with, as the Enlightenment *philosophes* did, only an animal bloodbath which religious tradition had precariously distanced us from. So what was really needed for stability and peace, he thought, was faith and fear in the face of unfathomable mystery, best maintained by the holy trinity of King, Pope, and Hangman. Or perhaps, as Mendelssohn had advocated on behalf of the Enlightenment, religion needed to be regulated by reason, just like everything else.

Although Kant refused to take sides in the dispute between Jacobi and Mendelsohn (both tried to enlist his support), his revolutionary new 'transcendental idealism' was drawn into the ensuing debate, thereby triggering Obereit's contribution. Kant had argued that the ultimate reality of 'things-in-themselves' was unknowable, and that everything we can experience in space and time was just a limited appearance of that reality, one made possible by the processing powers of the human mind. As Obereit saw it, this prevented Metaphysics from leading Humanity to the true reality where God resides, and in which there was hope for salvation.

So we can now understand the plot of Obereit's book. The Nihilism driving Metaphysics to desperation had been produced by Kant's idealism blocking access to true reality, leaving Humanity with only the nothingness of mere appearance. With access to true reality blocked, Humanity would find itself confined by Nihilism to the 'vanity of vanities' which mortal life amounts to, according to Ecclesiastes. When Nihilism first speaks, it's like the devilish snake in the Garden of Eden, luring us away from Metaphysics and tempting us to resign ourselves to a pointless life of toil, in which mortal life is all we acknowledge – 'Work, work you must, for bread and for the poor, who multiply daily', says Nihilism, rather sensibly you might think.[3] But Obereit finds an intuition of Eternity, beyond the intuitions of space and time which Kant restricted us to, which allows Metaphysics to do its job for Humanity once more. So Nihilism's scheme comes to nothing.

When the word next occurs, it's used in Obereit's sense, namely as a product of idealism blotting out true reality. This was in a book about Kant's philosophy by Daniel Jenische (1762–1804?), a preacher who disappeared in mysterious circumstances, hence the question mark. The connection to atheism is explicitly made: idealism leads us to 'atheism and nihilism', he says.[4] That was in 1796, but three years earlier in France – the year Louis XVI lost his head to Madame Guillotine – a poet called Pierre Jean-Baptiste Chaussard defined a 'nihilist' as someone who lacks political opinion. Probably an independent development, this gave 'nihilism' and 'nihilist' a degree of independence for a while, since Chaussard's word quickly caught on as a term of abuse against free-thinking young intellectuals. But the context in which the need was felt for such a word is plain enough. In a dictionary of new French words from 1801, a 'nihilist' is defined as, 'One who does not believe in anything.

A fine product of the evil philosophy that flaunts itself in the fat *Dictionnaire encyclopédique*'.[5] This 'fat' encyclopaedia (28 volumes) was one of the great products of the French Enlightenment – an attempt to reorganise human knowledge on secular and rational grounds, taking it out of the hands of the church. It contains entries by Voltaire, Rousseau, Holbach, and other leading *philosophes*, on history, politics, economics, philosophy, science, medicine, music, literature ... you name it. Digest all that learning and you'd end up not believing *in* anything (but believing lots of things): you'd end up a nihilist.

Back in Germany, the next accusation of 'nihilism' was made by Old Fritz in the next public controversy he waded into. The accusation wasn't made against Kant's idealism this time, but rather that of J.G. Fichte, who was that rarest of rarities: a major figure in the history of philosophy who came from a peasant background. After a schooling paid for by a local Baron who spotted his talents, Fichte became a disciple of Kant – he named his son after him, 'Immanuel' – before breaking away to become, as the great historian of ideas Isaiah Berlin put it, 'the true father of Romanticism'.[6]

Romanticism arose in Germany as a Counter-Enlightenment movement which, according to Berlin's analysis, was a rebellion against French cultural dominance. Like the *Sturm und Drang* (storm and stress) movement in the arts which preceded it, it celebrated passion, creativity, imagination, and originality. From the romantic point of view, the problem with the Enlightenment was that it promoted a shallow, one-size-fits-all conformity. Its imperialist goal of perfecting life in accordance with a universal rationality ignored the cultural and historical differences which provide the wellsprings of innovation, and blinded us to the sometimes beautiful and sometimes terrifying mysteries of reality – in this latter concern, it had much in common with traditional religious opposition to Enlightenment.

Fichte's initial attraction to Kant's idealism was as a defence against materialism, figuring that if Kant was right that true reality is unknowable, there could be no reason to believe it. Like Obereit and Janische, however, the idea of being out of touch with true reality disturbed him. His solution was to find true reality in his own creative free will, itself bounded by God's infinite will. Acts of will 'posited' the external world we find surrounding us, basically through an individual willpower saying to itself: 'not me'. This romantic idea of freedom and imagination being at the heart of reality earned Fichte a devoted following in Jena, where he worked as a philosophy lecturer and lived in a very nice house (which is now a museum you can visit). But all that ended when he was accused of atheism and fired. In Fichte's furious response, he says that to call him an atheist was the same as saying 'you are no more than an animal', but that his accusers were the real animals, since they were incapable of understanding his sophisticated philosophy.[7]

In the controversy that followed, Jacobi wrote letters to Fichte, then published them (with permission – no deaths this time). He praises him as the 'King' of speculative reason, better even than Kant, and defends him against the charge of atheism. But the support is double-edged, because the onus is that speculative reason leads us dangerously astray, namely to nihilism. It leads to the building of castles in the air, by taking reality for what can be known perfectly, like geometrical figures. Just like maths, Fichte's philosophy is too abstract to be atheist – but for the same reason, can't be theist either. He says that Fichte's achievement was to improve and perfect Spinozism (which Jacobi was famous for opposing, of course) by showing that materialism leads to idealism. So rather than trying to make complete sense of material nature, thereby turning it into Spinoza's all-encompassing God, Fichte had seen that the human will provides its own material for speculative philosophers, with the natural world only a consequence of its productive imagination. And so by conceiving self-contemplating mental activity as the true reality, Fichte had turned the human will into a kind of god. But he was a pious man with God in his heart, Jacobi assures us, so if there were atheistic implications, this was only 'the bungling of the artist'.

Still, the bungling was disastrous. After satirising Fichte's philosophy as conceiving a stocking as a self-weaving 'thread' of thought, Jacobi traces the root of the problem to forgetting about purpose, since a stocking can't be understood 'without reference to, and for the purpose of, a human leg'. Jacobi 'flies into a rage' when this kind of purposeless thinking is applied to life itself, so as to portray it as a 'Danaidic' existence (the Danaids of Greek mythology pointlessly poured water into a leaky tub). He 'shudders in horror and fright' to think of Fichte's 'purely self-intending and self-contemplating activity' existing 'without inheritance, point of departure, purpose, or point of arrival'. By trying to find true reality through abstract reasoning, then, Fichte's big mistake was to reason without guidance from God's truth, to which reason is 'exclusively directed as to its ultimate goal'. The result was that Fichte found only a meaningless abstraction of his own imagination – a true reality of nothingness, with nothing outside it. To avoid this nihilism, he should have sought the basis of reason not in himself – the reasoning 'I' – but in 'the "More than I"! the "Better than I"!' Jacobi, who doesn't think he would exist without God, and '*would not want to*', finds that his own reason 'instinctively teaches me: God' and 'compels me to believe in the incomprehensible'.[8]

The message is clear: if you turn your back on God's purpose by pursuing reason independently, you'll reason everything away and believe in nothing. Obereit and Jenische thought Kant's idealism blotted out God's meaningful reality, while Jacobi thought Fichte's more radical version obliterated it. In each case, idealism leads to nihilism by trapping us in our own minds. Idealism and materialism were just as bad because a mind-constituted reality was as distant from God's purpose as one made of atoms, and both resulted from letting independent reasoning and the desire for absolute knowledge run amuck. Metaphysicians couldn't win – they should've stuck with theology. And what really fired the emotions was that if we started believing these new-fangled ideas, we'd end up confined to Ecclesiastes' 'vanity of vanities'. The French revolutionary sense of 'nihilist' shows the same concern, just with a political edge, since free-thinking about God's purpose threatened traditional political and cultural institutions. Remove the context of German philosophy and the French Revolution, and the core meaning of 'nihilism' is the view that there's no meaning of life.

Jacobi accused Fichte of nihilism in 1799, the same year the iconic phrase, 'the meaning of life', was first published – at the end of Friedrich Schlegel's influential novel, *Lucinde*. Fichte was living at Schlegel's place at the time, having just lost his job, and was writing a popular presentation of his ideas to make it clear that he thought God's infinite will gave 'meaning, purpose and value' to reality; he didn't want the 'animals' misunderstanding him again. The phrase had already been used the previous year, in a notebook of one of the other 'Jena Romantics', called Novalis – so cool he gave himself a one-word moniker. Novalis wrote that, 'Only an artist can divine the meaning of life', which cuts to the heart of the romantic sensibility. The 'meaning of life' was now something you needed to search for, like a detective, and artistic sensibilities were required. Schlegel presents it as something you decipher from the code of nature, written in 'mysterious hieroglyphs on flowers and stars', and Novalis emphasised the creative angle, saying that, 'We live in a colossal novel (writ large and small)'. The idea of God as the 'author' of the 'book of life' goes back to medieval times, but the idea of reading that book, let alone making your own contribution, was new and thoroughly romantic. Inspired by Fichte's philosophy, the idea was to look for clues about God's big meaning, then create our own stories to harmonise with it. So as soon as the meaning of life was named, amid fear of nihilism, the scene was set for it to become a secular project. People still look inside themselves to try to discover the meaning of their lives, while atheist philosophers try to work out the universal formula which everyone should follow.[9]

'The meaning of life' and 'nihilism' – the good and bad twins – started to catch on in the first half of the 19th century. There were no great innovations, just a gradual distancing from concerns about idealism, with nihilism now blamed on the likes of science and socialism, as churchmen worried that the moral fabric of Christian society was being degraded by a wanton pursuit of knowledge, or social justice, that left impressionable young people in a moral vacuum. A big innovation that did occur, however, was the invention of existentialism by Danish philosopher Søren Kierkegaard. Kierkegaard was concerned about the meaning of life, and uses that terminology, but he didn't use 'nihilism'.[10] He did, however, have lots to say about 'levelling'. Subsequent philosophers have equated nihilism with levelling – it continues to this day – which is a shame both because it muddies the waters, and because 'levelling', unlike 'nihilism', is an appropriate label for what Kierkegaard had in mind.

Kierkegaard was concerned about passion draining from modern life, which was becoming too trivial and superficial for his likings – his native Copenhagen was home to the world's first theme park, Tivoli Gardens, which he despised. He saw life becoming too easy and people too wishy-washy, everything levelling-out to become uniformly unexceptional. His solution was to recapture the fervour of Christianity, seeing faith as an emotional struggle for authentic existence in the face of an inscrutable and capricious God. Whenever you hear an author berating the superficial nihilism of this or that aspect of modern life, they've probably got levelling in mind.

Then, there was a surprising development in 1860s Russia – nihilism became the good guy. The context was that Russia had been crushed in the Crimean war which ended in 1856. The country found itself in a desperate state, and among widespread dissatisfaction, the 80% of Russia's population who lived in serfdom were emancipated. Young intellectuals who felt solidarity with the ex-serfs wanted more reforms, and Ivan Turgenev's novel, *Fathers and Sons*, gave them a banner to march under: 'nihilism'. The hero of the novel, Bazarov, says that a nihilist is someone who 'bows down to no authority, who takes no single principle on trust, however much respect be attached to that principle'. He promotes science and social change, and tells us that nihilists base their conduct on 'what we recognise as useful', and that the 'most useful course of action at present is to reject'.[11] Inspired by this ideal, the nihilist movement started pressing for more freedoms, more knowledge, and less religious tradition. Many were women, who wanted privileges such as being allowed to go to university – nihilism was an early feminist movement. This certainly wasn't part of Kierkegaard's agenda for putting the spark back into life, since he strongly opposed women's liberation. The nihilist movement didn't last long, however, and when religious reactionaries associated it with later groups engaged in revolutionary acts of terror, they made nihilism seem worse than ever.

The next major development, and the one that cast the biggest shadow over discussions of nihilism in the 20th century, is that Friedrich Nietzsche made it a theme of his philosophy in the 1880s. His main innovation was to make nihilism seem like a problem for atheists – it had previously only been a problem for religious beliefs and institutions. He was also responsible for fuzzing the concept up, which wasn't his fault, since most of what he said about it is in notebooks that weren't meant for publication. The ideas he jotted down about 'nihilism' point in many directions.

Sometimes nihilism is good – it could be a *'divine way of thinking'* if it means admitting to yourself 'the necessity of lies', since there's no true reality anyway, as Nietzsche thought. Sometimes, he welcomes nihilism as a destructive force set to sweep away the Christian order he so detested. He even tells us that he himself was a nihilist for most of his life, 'the first perfect nihilist of Europe', having only 'recently' outgrown it in 1887; less than two years before he developed dementia and never recovered. Yet, most of his notes present nihilism as a disease of the soul infecting European culture, and much else besides, which resulted from everyone supposedly doing what Kierkegaard thought they should do, but very rarely did, namely 'become nothing before God'.[12] Having thereby invested everything worthwhile in a fiction, Nietzsche thought, they'd be left with nothing when atheism burst the bubble – and only he had foreseen the impending disaster. Nevertheless, he thought special, strong-willed people could overcome nihilism to make life meaningful again – which was just to invoke the original romantic notion of the meaning of life, except without clues from God this time.

A Brief History of Nihilism 23

Just as Kierkegaard thought God's meaning should be our all-consuming passion, Nietzsche thought atheists should be passionate about making their own. Kierkegaard saw this passion in Christ and the early saints, while Nietzsche saw it in anyone who overcame conservative opposition to leave their own original mark on the world. Both hated levelling, an idea which colours many of Nietzsche's notes on nihilism – one of nihilism's 'causes', for instance, was the 'lower species', or 'herd', losing its 'modesty' and 'blow[ing] up its needs into cosmic and metaphysical values' such that 'the whole of existence is vulgarized'.[13] Another notion related to levelling, but which often creeps into discussions of nihilism, is Nietzsche's description of 'the last man' – a horrifying (to him) vision of a future where the 'herd' completely takes over, everyone is happy, poverty and extreme wealth have been eliminated, and people enjoy their work. But this was in an earlier, published book, and he doesn't call it 'nihilism' – he was probably a nihilist at the time, by his own reckoning.[14]

In the 20th century, discussion of nihilism spread far and wide. Sometimes, it was a force of decline driving civilisation to destruction – nihilism was blamed for both world wars – while sometimes it was a liberating force that offered new opportunities. Since this is a brief history, however, we'll only touch on one more contributor: Martin Heidegger, whose status as one of the century's most important philosophers, combined with his involvement with the Nazi regime (he sported a Hitler-moustache for a while), has made him an endless source of fascination. Heidegger's main statement about nihilism was composed between 1940 and 1946. By the time he'd finished, the Nazis had lost and Germany was in ruins.

Focusing on Nietzsche's statement that nihilism means 'the highest values devaluate themselves', Heidegger conceives nihilism as a historical process, one stretching back to the birth of metaphysics in Ancient Greece. And focusing on Nietzsche's solution, namely a 'revaluation of all values' enacted by the 'will to power' of the better class of people he prophesised, Heidegger comes to the conclusion that Nietzsche was part of the problem. The problem was metaphysics, with Nietzsche's philosophy being 'the fulfilment of Western metaphysics in general'. Sound familiar? Think back to the double-edged compliment Jacobi paid to Fichte: Fichte's the best metaphysician around, but metaphysics leads you to nihilism.

Heidegger became famous in the 1920s for asking 'the question of the meaning of Being', and since he asked it by focusing on everyday life, this was a variant on asking about the meaning of life. His solution was the romantic one mixed with some Kierkegaard: strong emotions would wake us up from the spell of the mindless mob, so we could forge our own authentic paths. By the time Heidegger was preoccupied with Nietzsche and nihilism, however, he'd started to think a more passive approach was called for. Actively interrogating reality – metaphysics – had initiated the process of forgetting about Being, with which he equated nihilism. This process had made everything seem like an object in relation to the human will interrogating it, thereby leading to an understanding of reality as something you manipulate – a scientific understanding which produced the bombs dropping on Germany. Nietzsche's strong-willed types bending reality to their will was just the subjective flipside of this metaphysical understanding – rather as Jacobi had said that materialism and idealism amount to the same – and the result was that we'd found ourselves 'homeless' on our own planet, no longer sensitive to the meaning of our lives within it, as we pointlessly undertook its 'global conquest' and tried to 'thrust into outer space'.[15] Heidegger's quest to remember the point of our existence by interpreting texts pre-dating the metaphysics that produced nihilism, or by otherwise trying to listen to the voice of Being, became increasingly mystical as he got older.

So what, if anything, is to be made of this history? Reading between the lines, perhaps the history of nihilism is just the history of people gradually coming to terms with the realisation that there's no good reason to suppose that we live in a reality God designed, with a specific purpose to fulfil, and an afterlife to look forward to. Coming to see this for the first time was shocking, of course, and since this intellectual development combined with economic, technological, and social developments which destabilised the traditional religious structure of life, nihilism caused much anxiety. Early atheists still wanted their lives to be meaningful, because they still had one foot in the religious framework – rejecting God and the afterlife was easier than rejecting the idea that you, yourself, had a cosmically worthwhile existence. But without God to endow the cosmic meaning, the task of conjuring it up yourself seemed daunting (because it's impossible). As progress continued, snobbery provoked by the working classes starting to get a better deal merged with this philosophical concern, since *they* obviously weren't taking it seriously enough; more conspicuous now they'd forgotten their place, their gross manners seemed to indicate decay. And thus, nihilism started to seem like a poisonous wind blowing through history. But there's nothing wrong with nihilism – it can't help being true and we were bound to notice the void eventually.[16]

Notes

1. Götze, *De Nonismo et Nihilismo in Theologia*, 609–11. The translation of this extract is by Zo Hoida. Götze's book was never reprinted but exists online.
2. Jacobi, *The Main Philosophical Writings and the Novel Allwill*, 88.
3. Quoted and translated by Giesbers, 'The Wall or the Door: German Realism around 1800', which is available for free online. We found it very helpful for understanding Obereit.
4. Jenische, *über Grund*, 203. It's easy to find online.
5. Goudsblom, *Nihilism and Culture*, 3. We relied on this book in many places for this chapter.
6. Berlin, *The Crooked Timber of Humanity*, 239.
7. Fichte's 'Appeal to the Public', 93.
8. Jacobi, *The Main Philosophical Writings and the Novel Allwill*, 497.
9. See Leach and Tartaglia, 'The Blue Flower', 274–83.
10. Not that we could find anyway – and we checked with a Kierkegaard scholar.
11. Turgenev, *Fathers and Sons*, 23, 49. We've used the Penguin Classics version, with Bazarov explaining that a nihilist is a 'man who …', but other versions say 'person' or 'someone'. The translations vary a lot. Petrov opts for 'person' and also says that *Fathers and Children* is a more literal translation of the title; see '"Strike Out, Right and Left!"', 73–4.
12. Kierkegaard, *The Lily in the Field and the Bird in the Air* (1849), 333.
13. The quotes about nihilism from Nietzsche's notebooks are in Book One ('European Nihilism') of *The Will to Power*.
14. Nietzsche described the 'last' or 'ultimate' man in *Thus Spake Zarathustra*.
15. Heidegger, *Nietzsche, Vols. III & IV*, 138, 248. We're discussing Vol. IV ('Nihilism').
16. For help with some of the research, and especially the languages, we'd like to thank Sophie Allen, Maria Brosoveanu, Stephen Leach, and Martin Müller.

Bibliography

Berlin, Isaiah. *The Crooked Timber of Humanity*. London: Pimlico, 2013.
Fichte, Johann Gottlieb. 'Appeal to the Public'. In *J.G. Fichte and the Atheism Dispute*, 85–126. Edited by Yolanda Estes and Curtis Bowman. Farnham: Ashgate, 2010.
Giesbers, Tom. 'The Wall or the Door: German Realism around 1800'. PhD diss. Universiteit Utrecht, 2017.
Götze, Friedrich Lebrecht. *De Nonismo et Nihilismo in Theologia*. Chemnitii: Sumptibus Joh. Christ. & Joh. David. Stoesselii, cygneæ, ex officina Joh. Frid. Hoefferi, 1733.
Goudsblom, Johan. *Nihilism and Culture*. Oxford: Basil Blackwell, 1980.
Heidegger, Martin. *Nietzsche, Vols. III & IV*. Edited by David Farrell Krell and translated by Frank Capuzzi. New York: Harper Collins, 1991.

Jacobi, Friedrich Heinrich. *The Main Philosophical Writings and the Novel Allwill*. Edited and translated by George di Giovanni. Montreal: McGill-Queen's University Press, 1994.

Jenische, Daniel. *Über Grund Und Werth Der Entdeckungen Des Herrn Professor Kant in Der Metaphysik, Moral Und Aesthetik*. Berlin: Friedrich Vieweg dem älteren, 1976.

Kierkegaard, Soren. *The Lily in the Field and the Bird in the Air* (1849). In *The Essential Kierkegaard*, 333–8. Edited by Howard V. Hong and Edna H. Hong. New Jersey: Princeton University Press, 2000.

Leach, Stephen and James Tartaglia. 'The Blue Flower'. In *The Meaning of Life and the Great Philosophers*, 274–83. Edited by Stephen Leach and James Tartaglia. London: Routledge, 2018.

Nietzsche, Friedrich. *The Will to Power*. Translated by Walter Kaufmann and R.J. Hollingdale. New York: Vintage Books, 1967.

Nietzsche, Friedrich. *Thus Spake Zarathustra*. Translated by Thomas Common. New York: Dover Publications, 1999.

Petrov, Kristian. '"Strike Out, Right and Left!": A Conceptual-Historical Analysis of 1860s Russian Nihilism and Its Notion of Negation', *Studies in East European Thought*, 71 (2019): 73–97.

Turgenev, Ivan. *Fathers and Sons*. Translated by Peter Carson. London: Penguin Classics, 2009.

3 Nil Desperandum

Pessimism has become heavily embroiled with nihilism; the terms are sometimes even used as synonyms nowadays. But if you give 'nihilism' a clear sense, the one best-rooted in its history, you see that it's completely different. The nihilist view that there's no meaning of life – none whatsoever – should obviously not be confused with the view that there's an awful, terrible meaning of life. And unless you start from the particular religious premise that cosmic meaning is required for a good life, then there's no reason nihilism should lead you to pessimism. The fact that a very unhappy person doesn't care about much in their life, and hence doesn't sense much good meaning in it, provides them with no clue to the nature of reality – sadness doesn't grant special ability to bust through illusion, you need a clear head for that. You'd be suspicious of a treatise on the unmitigated joys of life written by somebody honeymooning on an idyllic tropical island with the love of their life, so the fact that deeply pessimistic philosophies are usually the product of unhappy people is a perfectly reasonable ground for suspicion. They're the people who might *want* to portray human life in gloomy colours. No reasonable person would intend to reason themselves into unhappiness, but if you're already miserable, you might want to spread the pain by universalising it; with the added bonus that you get to feel rather clever for noticing the universal suffering that the stupid, happy masses overlook. But wanting something to be true isn't a good reason for thinking it is.

Pessimism is essentially a value judgement. And it was Nietzsche, that 'first perfect nihilist of Europe', who said that, 'value judgements concerning life, for or against, can in the last resort never be true', they are 'stupidities', and that for 'a philosopher to see a problem in the value of life thus even constitutes an objection to him, a question-mark as to his wisdom'.[1] He was bang on. Value judgements are at home in the thick of life, where they allow us to say, for example, that the party was *good*, but that missing it because you had flu was *bad*. Try to say that human life itself is bad, however, and the meaning of 'bad' is liable to be replaced by gloomy hot air. Nihilism isn't a value judgement – if it's true, then it states a fact, on a par with 'the 300 ml capacity glass contains 150 ml of water'. Only pessimism makes the value judgement that it's half-empty.

Pessimism originates as a distinctive brand of philosophy only in modern times, not long after the meaning of life and nihilism were named, and it stems from the same group of German philosophers. There's plenty of pessimism in earlier authors, of course, such as in the bitter sweet moods conjured up by the Roman poet Horace, or the grim appraisals of the trials and tribulations of life to be found in Stoic philosophers, while they teach us how to live like immovable rocks which the waves of misfortune will simply wash over. Just like optimism, pessimism is part of human life and sometimes appropriate – if you see that something bad is about to happen, then an optimistic refusal to face the facts is annoying, and, if there's anything that can be done about it, counterproductive. But the kind of pessimism that completely condemns human life, and has gone nuclear with the absurd proposal that we must endeavour to bring it to an end, is very much a modern phenomenon.

It is often traced back to the Italian poet Giacomo Leopardi (1798–1837), who suffered throughout his short life from a battery of debilitating illnesses, as well as from ultra-religious parents, bereavement, and poverty – before he was struck down by cholera. He also suffered from a 'boredom' which he said 'plagues and racks me like a terrible pain' – these days we would call it depression. Nevertheless, he found consolation in reading and writing about it, saying that works which 'capture exactly the nothingness of things, or vividly reveal and make us feel life's inevitable unhappiness, or express the most acute hopelessness ... are always a source of consolation and renewed enthusiasm' – albeit only 'momentarily'.

Influenced by materialist philosophers like Holbach, and probably an atheist himself (although he's said to have received confession on his deathbed), Leopardi was concerned by the onslaught of reason the Enlightenment had unleashed; the same concern Jacobi showed in his opposition to nihilism. As Leopardi saw it, reason had been okay in the olden days, when it restricted its ambitions to helping us get around in the natural world, but by overextending itself, it was no longer serving to make us happy – which is its only proper purpose – but rather unhappy.

The main problem, he thought, is that our desire is always for infinite pleasure, but reason had revealed that we'll never get it. As he explains,

> If you desire to possess a horse, it seems to you that you desire it as a horse and as a particular pleasure. But in fact you desire it as an abstract and unlimited pleasure. When you then find yourself in possession of the horse, you encounter a pleasure that is necessarily restricted, and, because of the unsatisfied state of your actual desire, you sense a feeling of emptiness in your soul.

Is that right? Perhaps the 'necessarily restricted' pleasure of getting the horse would be just fine and dandy, and once you'd ridden it around, petted it, and showed it off to your friends, you wouldn't in fact be left with a 'feeling of emptiness in your soul', just satisfaction and eagerness for the next day of fun with your four-legged friend. However, if you'd once expected an eternal afterlife of satisfaction provided by the Christian meaning of life, and had since been disillusioned by learning so much (Leopardi's voracious reading habits left him blind in one eye), then perhaps you might feel that way.

Despite everything life threw at him, however, Leopardi didn't despair in his philosophy, saying that, 'I believe it to be much worthier of the human being and of magnanimous despair to laugh at our common ills rather than sighing, weeping and screeching together with the others and instigating them to do the same'. Much like Nietzsche, who greatly admired him, Leopardi had the positive aim of escaping the cul-de-sac which he thought reason had led us to, proposing that human imagination might play the key role in leading reason back to happiness – rather as the original romantics thought it would lead us to God's meaning. It was another of Leopardi's admirers, Arthur Schopenhauer, who began the 'weeping', 'screeching', and 'instigating' tradition of pessimism.[2]

Schopenhauer was the main philosophical influence on Nietzsche, although he ultimately turned against him; he probably had Schopenhauer in mind when he denounced philosophers who see a problem in the value of life. Schopenhauer, who studied under Fichte for a time, would have known all about the controversies over atheism and nihilism we talked about in the previous chapter. Unperturbed, Schopenhauer openly endorsed atheism and nihilism in his main work, *The World as Will and Representation*, first published in 1818; 'nihilism' isn't one of his words, but he's quite clear that life and reality generally are meaningless. The book was largely ignored, much to his embitterment, but he did live to see it catch on in his final years (he died in 1860), when it kicked off a pessimism controversy which ran on for decades.

Just like Fichte, Schopenhauer was a disciple of Kant who couldn't tolerate the Kantian conclusion that ultimate reality is unknowable. He conceived the task of finding out what it is as akin to the way physical scientists work out the nature of unobservable particles on the basis of what they can observe. And the key observation which had been overlooked, he thought, was that each of us experiences our own bodies both from the inside and the outside – you can both see your hand reaching out to grab something, and feel it as a willed action from the inside. What exactly he made of this remains a subject of scholarly debate. Sometimes, he suggests that he's made the discovery – ultimate reality is will! Sometimes, he seems only to be saying that this is the best sense human beings can make of it. Neither makes an awful lot of sense, because according to his Kantian idealist principles, willing can't be the ultimate reality since it happens in time, and everything in time is a mere representation. But then why think the inside representations of our bodies willing are any more accurate than the outside representations of them as physical objects moving? In any case, Schopenhauer convinced himself that ultimate reality is especially will-like and projected this insight across the whole cosmos, seeing magnets attracting and repelling each other as manifestations of will, for instance.

He also projects this insight onto human life, and when combined with his atheism – which he consistently follows through to nihilism – modern pessimism was born. Willing is ultimately pointless, he thinks: 'Every individual act has a purpose or end; willing as a whole has no end in view'. And the problem with that, as he sees it, is that all this willing produces misery and horror, because the willing can't stop but has nowhere to go. With no meaning of life to arrive at, it 'swings like a pendulum' and we're stuck in 'constant transition from desire to satisfaction, and from that to a fresh desire'. But the satisfaction is always disappointing, and hence just as painful as the lack you feel when desiring something you don't have – it hurts when you want it and hurts when you get it. Try to break out of the cycle and it's even worse, because then you're trying to frustrate the nature of reality itself (or something like it) and you end up with 'a fearful, life-destroying boredom, a lifeless longing without a definite object, a deadening languor'; it seems more than likely that Schopenhauer was describing his depression here. He bolsters his case for despair with some reflections on animal life, with a memorable example being a report he heard about giant turtles being torn apart by wild dogs, with the dogs then torn apart by opportunist tigers. Influenced by the pre-Darwinian discussion of evolution going on at that time, Schopenhauer sees the natural struggle for survival as an outside representation of the pointless will torturing itself.[3]

Schopenhauer's denouncement of life relies on a jaundiced and distorted description of it, however, which seems to be the key feature of the tradition he inaugurated. There needn't be anything even slightly unpleasant about wanting something – it's often exciting, as you eagerly beaver away to get what you're after, or just wait in keen anticipation. And when you do get what you want, it needn't be disappointing – it can be deeply satisfying, with the satisfaction ranging from fleeting gratification that doesn't have time to go sour, to something that endures for the rest of your life, like a friendship or a cherished achievement. When we disengage – to just space out, or chill at the beach – we're not all struck by a 'deadening languor'. Our lives are rarely even able to 'swing like a pendulum', in fact, because that would require a completely one-tracked dedication to a single project at a time, as a pendulum is always either swinging up or down. But our lives are typically filled with loads of different interweaving projects.

Nothing about Schopenhauer's description of life rings true for us – but maybe it did for him. His mother, a popular author and socialite, found her son intolerably gloomy as a child; and presumably he hadn't been persuaded by the arguments to be found in his *magnum opus* at that point. (The same can be said of the latest manifestation of this tradition, contemporary philosopher David Benatar – who we'll discuss later – who revealed in an interview that he's known his 'truth' since childhood.) Schopenhauer later took revenge on the mother he couldn't get along with by penning some of the most ludicrous misogyny the world's ever seen: women's bodies, unlike men's, are objectively revolting, for example, and the reason they're good at looking after children is that their minds are congenitally childlike. It's hard to trust Schopenhauer's objectivity concerning half of the human race, at least, and it doesn't look like he did any better with the whole thing.

Schopenhauer got people thinking about whether life is worth living in the latter half of the 19th century – and it continues to this day in some quarters. As historian of philosophy Frederick

Beiser has noted, this was a new, atheistic version of the Problem of Evil.[4] That's the argument that an all-powerful and all-good God wouldn't allow the suffering we see in the world, so there can't be one. Atheists now started to see suffering as a reason not to question God, but life, by asking whether the good times outweigh the bad. The religious inspiration is clear enough, because only on the assumption that the loss of God's meaning devalues life, would the existence of suffering suddenly seem to call for a cost-benefit analysis – atheism was new, suffering wasn't. But once you've stopped evaluating life against its higher meaning, you don't have to evaluate it at all – reality doesn't require this of us. We can stick to evaluating the quality of football games or the utility of political summits, where the limited context makes sensible evaluation possible. We can't perform a cost-benefit analysis of the pains and pleasures in human life – not even in principle – because the whole idea is completely confused. The correct analysis will always elude us, just as the meaning of life did.

To see this, put a number to the pain or pleasure you get from reading this paragraph. So that we can compare, let's make it −10 for the worst you've ever felt, 0 for so-so, and 10 for maximally awesome. Now rate how you felt when you woke up this morning. You probably can't remember, so let's stick with your number for this paragraph. We'd give the writing of it a 3, so compare that with your number for reading it – was that enlightening? Now how about rating every day of your life – not just the past ones, but the future ones too – and doing the same for all the billions of people currently alive, all the past lives, and all the future ones too. Forget precision, and just ask if that's something you can estimate? No it's not, because it's the wrong way to think about life. Here are three reasons why.

Firstly, conscious experience isn't something that's always pleasurable or painful, one or the other. Unless reading our paragraph particularly irritated you, you'll find the notion of pain alien to what you experienced – you were lost in a world of thought to which notions of pleasure and pain just don't apply. Even if you were irritated, any comparison to episodes of stepping on nails is obviously very loose – the irritation probably consisted in rehearsing objections in your mind. Secondly, you can't even measure the clear-cut cases of pain and pleasure, because they're subjective conscious experiences. The individual having them can make comparisons – 'I didn't enjoy that as much as the last time I visited this restaurant' – but the idea of an absolute measure for intersubjective comparison and then counting up, a special kind of ruler, just doesn't make sense. And thirdly, whoever said that whether life is worth living is determined by the amount of pleasure it contains? If pleasure is all you're interested in, then you might think that a drug addict has a valuable life, but a woman who works hard to support her family doesn't. That might indeed be your evaluation, but it wouldn't be everyone's – and there's no universal evaluation if there's no meaning of life. Schopenhauer thought that he suffered much more than he enjoyed. But he kept on labouring away at his philosophy, wishing people would acknowledge his genius. Perhaps he didn't evaluate his own life in terms of pain and pleasure, then, but rather in terms of the work he produced. He wouldn't have been the first and wasn't the last. The endlessly ground-breaking musician John Zorn once said that, 'Happiness is for children and yuppies. I'm not striving for happiness, I'm trying to get some work done'.

Pessimistic philosophy of this kind begins in the thought that without a meaning of life, the value of human life is placed into question; in other words, in an erroneous and religiously inspired reaction to nihilism. It's interesting to see where it led. The worst horror arrived almost immediately, with the true heir to Schopenhauer, Eduard von Hartmann. His three-volume *Philosophy of the Unconscious* (1869) is an uneasy mix of metaphysics, a critique of Darwin's theory of evolution (to make way for his own variety of evolution), and fanciful speculation based on the brain science of his day. Above all, however, it is an argument for collective suicide. To get to this outcome as quickly as possible, he thought, we needed to speed up evolution. First of all, those 'incapable of competition with the white race' must be dispensed with as quickly as possible, to make way for more ferocious struggles to break out between 'different stocks within the highest race' – the 'more merciless' the process, the 'more advantageous for the progression of the race'.[5] Eventually, those who were left would have such big brains that they'd all recognise the need for a suicide pact. Then, the tragedy of the human race would be brought to an end and reality would be returned to harmony. As American philosopher Ellen Mitchell put it, back in 1886,

> No touch of compassion or human sympathy relieves the picture that he draws. It almost seems as if he felt a kind of cold joy in building up a logical system of thought that will shatter every human hope and trust.[6]

It does indeed. His wife seems to have loved him, however; she carried on defending his views even when she was a widow.

It's particularly telling that when Hartmann describes the final stage of evolution, he refers back to Ecclesiastes; that's when 'finally all is recognised as "vanity of vanities"'. In that case perhaps we could skip straight to the end of the process by encouraging atheists to read the Bible. But Hartmann wasn't alone in seeing evolution as the meaning of life for atheists. As soon as Darwin's theory became a hot topic, so did the idea of 'perfecting' humanity with 'eugenics', which was named by Darwin's cousin, Francis Galton. Its popularity seriously waned after the atrocities of the Nazis, but it hasn't gone away; biologist Richard Dawkins, of 'God Delusion' fame, thinks that it's worth considering again, and people with eugenic sympathies have even made their way into the current UK government. What these people think the point of 'perfecting' the human race is, God only knows; as only God has ever known the meaning of life. Perhaps they think that we're all destined to merge into a big ball of cosmic pleasure, and that this outcome makes it worthwhile to cause division and suffering in the interim. Hartmann's mass suicide was supposed to make it all worthwhile in the end – and that's what meanings of life are always supposed to do.[7]

The current manifestation of the Schopenhauer-Hartmann tradition is provided by South African philosopher David Benatar. Like Hartmann, he calls for an end to humanity, albeit through the milder proposal that we stop having babies – 'anti-natalism', they call it. Hartmann thought that stupidity makes people think they're happy – that the cleverest are the saddest – and Benatar seems to agree. Noteworthy features of his works include assurances to the reader that he really means it, a lofty resignation to most people rejecting his conclusions, and concern that he might be doing something irresponsible. He is, after all, trying to persuade everyone that their lives are much worse than they realise .... not even worth living, since it would be 'Better Never to Have Been', as he announces in the title of one of his books. That catchy phrase is worth pausing over, because people's lives really can fall apart so irreparably that they wish they'd never been born; Thomas Hardy's tragic novel, *Jude The Obscure*, paints a disturbing portrait of someone like that. If there isn't a massive distinction to be drawn between tragic and ordinary lives, then that's a really big deal. Even if you were sure there isn't, the decent default would be to refrain from exploding the illusion, not just because you might be wrong, but because the immediate aim is to make people who feel alright come to think they shouldn't, and hence not feel alright anymore. Benatar's purported compassion for the unborn he wants to save from suffering – the bit that makes it all worthwhile in the end – raises the question of whether they'd agree with him. Some have indeed been persuaded, such as a man who'd already had two children by the time Benatar got to him – that'll be a nice thing for them to grow up knowing about their dad.[8] Most busy, working people, however, would regard the very existence of this discourse as firm evidence that philosophy is a decadent frivolity.

So what are his cast-iron arguments? Pains last longer, and are more intense, than pleasures; orgasms pass quickly, but chronic pain can last for years, he says. On the dubious assumption that this isn't comparing apples and oranges, are there really pains more intense than orgasm? You'd think you'd pass out very quickly. And isn't it perfectly normal to live many decades without chronic pain, while enjoying a healthy sex life, among many other things? According to Benatar, under the influence of the shrivelled cost-benefit conception of life which characterises this tradition, we overlook and unjustifiably dismiss the suffering that fills a normal day – there's hunger and thirst, and when we do something about it, 'the discomfort of discontented bladders and bowels'. There's 'thermal discomfort' too – feeling hot or cold – plus tiredness. Passing swiftly over the clear potential for a Monty Python sketch here, is it not obvious that the reason people ignore the feeling of needing to pee is because there's almost always something more interesting going on, and they're not silly enough to conceive that moment of their lives as defined by it; to *make* it defined by it, in fact, through the very act of focusing. And apart from these possibly original contributions, all we find in Benatar is a dutiful recital of Schopenhauer's pendulum argument, and, most of the time, a listing of the ills of human life which grown-ups already know about.

Benatar gets to the heart of what bothers him, we suspect, when he says that life is 'full of striving and struggle; there is much suffering and then we die', and so it is 'entirely reasonable to want there to be some point to the entire saga'. It's a source of deep regret, he thinks, that our lives make 'absolutely no difference to the rest of the universe'. How can he be sure that regretting that there's no meaning of life is a universal affliction? Sincere denials would be dismissed by him as products of the happy-illusion, no doubt, but he offers no argument as to why it *should* be universal, why it's 'entirely reasonable'. To be reasonable, there'd have to be a good reason why affecting the rest of the universe is a requirement of the good life. Blowing up large numbers of planets and stars presumably wouldn't be good enough, but in that case, what would be?[9]

Perhaps the answer is to be found within the existentialist offshoot of the pessimism tradition, and specifically, the work of Spanish philosopher Miguel de Unamuno, whose 1912 book, *The Tragic Sense of Life*, is still being read in the late 24th century – as viewers of *Star Trek: Picard* may have noticed. Unamuno's passionate philosophy opposes the ideal of 'truth for truth's sake', which he considers 'inhuman', and implores us to see philosophy as 'flesh and bone' people addressing each other about matters that personally affect them. He thinks that concern about the meaning of life has nothing to do with making our mark on reality, nor understanding why there is one, nor deciphering the cosmic meaning. Nobody's really interested in the 'why', he thinks, only the 'wherefore' – because we all want to live forever. Living with an inexhaustible appetite for life, the threat of death, and uncertainty about the afterlife is the 'personal and affective starting-point of all philosophy and all religion', he thinks – and this is what he calls 'the tragic sense of life'. He didn't see it as a reason to despair, however, and was sceptical of the pessimism label. Rather, he saw being honest about our instinctual drives as a source of inner strength, and an impetus to social action, in which he tirelessly engaged. After opposing the rise of Franco's dictatorship, he was placed under house arrest and died peacefully in his sleep.[10]

Maybe resistance to nihilism doesn't come from desire for just any old meaning of life, then, only the kind that promises eternal life. Maybe some people never really get over the childhood discovery that they're going to die one day, and that's the root of cosmic pessimism. Maybe there's a benefit to remembering our final destination, as both Unamuno and Heidegger thought, since it's energising, and reminds us not to whittle away our time on distractions. Or maybe there's no point dwelling on it. To start fretting that your amazing foreign holiday will come to an end the very moment the plane touches down at the airport, and never stop fretting until it actually does end, would be irrational; it won't prolong it, just spoil the time you have. So keep death always in mind, or just forget about it; one of the beauties of nihilism is that you can take or leave any such strategy for living. They're not recipes for the meaning of life, nor escape-routes from nihilism, but rather advice, plain and simple – and it always pays to be careful who you take advice from. A nihilist can be similarly flexible about whether they adopt a pessimistic or optimistic attitude to their lives, or just adjust to the situation, trying not to be either as a rule. Those who think that the deep and profound choice is always to be pessimistic will have to look elsewhere, since nihilism lends no metaphysical weight to pessimism, but rather removes it.

Notes

1. Nietzsche, *Twilight of the Idols and the Anti-Christ*, 40.
2. The quotes from Leopardi are taken from two online articles: Parks, 'The Great Disillusionist' and Sigurðsson, 'In Praise of Illusions: Giacomo Leopardi's Ultraphilosophy'.
3. Schopenhauer, *The World as Will and Representation, Vols. 1 & 2*, the quotes are from Vol. 1, 164–5 and 332; the tiger example is from Vol. 2, 354.
4. Beiser, *Weltschmerz: Pessimism in Germany, 1860–1900*, introduction.
5. von Hartmann, *Philosophy of the Unconscious*, quotes from Vol. 2, 12; and Vol. 3, 11.
6. Mitchell, 'The Philosophy of Pessimism', 193.
7. Interest in eugenics entered the UK government in 2020 via Dominic Cummings' appointment of Andrew Sabisky; Dawkins' controversial statement on eugenics was made in a November 2006 letter to the UK newspaper, *The Herald*.
8. Mentioned in Coates, *Anti-Natalism*, 126.
9. Benatar, *The Human Predicament*, 71 and 61–3.
10. Unamuno, *The Tragic Sense of Life*, 28–9 and 37.

Bibliography

Beiser, Frederick. *Weltschmerz: Pessimism in Germany, 1860–1900*. Oxford: Oxford University Press, 2016.

Benatar, David. *The Human Predicament*. Oxford: Oxford University Press, 2017.

Coates, Ken. *Anti-Natalism: Rejectionist Philosophy from Buddhism to Benatar*. Sarasota: First Edition Design Publishing, 2016.

Dawkins, Richard. 'From the Afterword'. *The Herald*, November 20, 2006. https://www.heraldscotland.com/news/12760676.from-the-afterword/

Hartmann, Edward von. *Philosophy of the Unconscious*. Translated by William Coupland. London: Kegan Paul, 1890.

Mitchell, Ellen. 'The Philosophy of Pessimism'. *Journal of Speculative Philosophy* 20, no. 2 (1886): 187–194.

Nietzsche, Friedrich. *Twilight of the Idols and the Anti-Christ*. Translated by R.J. Hollingdale and edited by Michael Tanner. London: Penguin, 1990.

Parks, Tim. 'The Great Disillusionist'. *Aeon*, November 13, 2018. https://aeon.co/essays/why-read-the-nihilistic-work-of-giacomo-leopardi-today

Schopenhauer, Arthur. *The World as Will and Representation, Vols. 1 and 2*. Translated by E.F.J. Payne. New York: Dover Publications, 1966.

Sigurðsson, Geir. 'In Praise of Illusions: Giacomo Leopardi's Ultraphilosophy'. *Nordicum-Mediterraneum* (e-journal) 5, no. 1 (2010). https://nome.unak.is/wordpress/05-1/articles51/in-praise-of-illusions-giacomo-leopardis-ultraphilosophy/

Unamuno, Miguel de. *The Tragic Sense of Life*. Translated by J.E. Crawford Flitch. London: Macmillan, 1931.

4 Nihil Sine Deo

Nihilism, or the idea that life has no cosmic meaning, entails that there's no grand design or blueprint to life, there's no deep reason for everything we do, and there's no heavenly gatekeeper evaluating the state of our souls to track whether we're exceeding moral expectations or failing miserably. This view has been historically engineered to appear as a very bad thing. But believing this is no reason for pessimism, as we've just been seeing, and it shouldn't threaten our many sources of social meaning, like family, job, pets, and passion projects. But maybe this reasoning remains insufficient to assuage *all* fears of meaninglessness. After all, it's difficult to shake off that nagging feeling that you're missing out, especially when there's a long historical tradition backing that impulse. Maybe that's why many of us are attracted to *Deus*-surrogates, be it nature, science, wacky forms of ethno-nationalism, authoritarian leaders, and the like: it's comforting to have something big and inspiring to believe in, and to have others galvanised by it too. The more powerful, the better.

Charles Taylor, Hubert Dreyfus, and Sean Kelly are three influential and strongly Heidegger-influenced philosophers who address these residual fears about nihilism in modernity. Heidegger, you'll remember, thought that the ancient Greeks set off a process which led to a purely manipulative conception of reality, and that because of this, we've now forgotten how to see the world as meaningful; Nietzsche, he thought, was the final stage in this process of forgetting. Taylor, Dreyfus, and Kelly represent what we'll call the 'moderate' view of nihilism. They still think that nihilism is a problem, but they're not quite so apocalyptic about it (not always, at least, since Dreyfus did think that nihilism may lead us to lose our bodies by spending too long on the internet). Their moderate view is that human beings can hope to overcome the threat of meaninglessness in a world still coming to grips with the secular turn. They view modern nihilism as a man-made problem. They believe that a retrieval or a rediscovery of some 'sacred' power can heal the negative existential consequences that arise from it.

The first step to understanding this view is figuring out how nihilism can be framed as a man-made problem, in the sense that we are responsible for the supposed badness of its consequences. For Taylor, Dreyfus, and Kelly, nihilism is tied to a 'human, all too human' (the title of one of Nietzsche's books) view of meaning, that is, the view that godless human beings can create or reproduce existential meaning on their own terms. Taylor, a Canadian philosopher who has a penchant for writing spectacularly big narratives like *Sources of the Self* (1989) and *A Secular Age* (2007), says that what sets Western modernity apart from other stages of human history is the erosion of its attachment to beings and things that have supernatural power and divine status; think Olympic deities, magic amulets, the rites of spring, and the Judeo-Christian God. Modern humans take less seriously the idea that offering a sacrifice to Artemis can help you win a marathon, that drinking a magic potion can protect you from demons, and that dancing in an annual fertility festival will bring rain and babies. Today, debating about God's existence over Thanksgiving makes for an uncomfortable conversation, but it's usually not life-threatening (whereas centuries ago, heretics were burned at the stake, and in the case of Fichte, it led to loss of employment and social bullying). In short, the supernatural and the divine have lost most of their existential *gravitas* and have diminished relevance, if any at all, in most of our everyday practices. But being cut off from traditional sources of existential value or meaning has various consequences, the moderates think, one of which includes our attention being redirected towards non-otherworldly sources, like the promise of technology, humanism, or the nation state. Taylor, Dreyfus, and Kelly think that these secular sources of meaning are generally both oriented and activated by the power of the human will (or freedom). Centring our lives around an 'anthropocentric' will, or radical freedom, they argue, has produced the social condition of modern nihilism. How exactly does this story go?

It helps to return to Nietzsche, the eternally recurring figure of this book, who transformed nihilism into a threat to believers and atheists alike. He treats nihilism as anthropocentric in its origins, which is a key premise that the moderates take as their point of departure. Nietzsche links nihilism to monotheism, or the belief in an all-powerful, all-knowing God which has shaped Western culture, society, and politics for over two millennia. Its metaphysics is dualistic: it pits a concept of the ideal against its flawed counterpart, e.g. the other-world vs. this-world, soul vs. body, truth vs. appearance, and good vs. evil. Nietzsche argues that monotheism promotes a 'slave' or 'herd' morality, or an ethics in which altruism, compassion, humility, and sacrifice are the highest values. He portrays these 'good' values as the life-denying values of the cowardly, sick, or unhappy Christians, employed to condemn the life-affirming values of the strong and the talented as 'evil' and to blame them for the miserable condition of the world. Monotheism, simply put, affirmed the weak and ordinary at the expense of human greatness.

But then the Enlightenment came along, a movement whose primary goal was to usher humanity's emergence from what Kant called its 'self-incurred immaturity'. Religion and political authority lost their blessed status in favour of human autonomy in the modern world, hence the popular line from Nietzsche's *The Gay Science* (1882): 'God is dead... And we have killed him'.[1] The collapse of Western society's deep structures of meaning created a profound crisis, signalling the transformation of the entire moral-spiritual outlook of the West, according to Nietzsche. This crisis and transformation, the consequence of human emancipation from monotheism, make up the character of nihilism. Nietzsche outlines two responses to the event of modern nihilism, either passive or active. The passive response means succumbing to existential vacuity. Passivity can also become destructive; since the passive nihilist has nothing left to value or affirm, the only human drive left to realise, should the nihilist choose not to kill himself, is the urge to destroy. The active response, however, is a sign of strength; this is the kind of nihilism Nietzsche himself claimed to have perfected. The active nihilist recognises that in the face of old and debased values, modern values have to be formulated to realise the needs of the modern man. And this is where Nietzsche gets unnerving: in his view, only persons of the 'noble' and 'higher' types will prosper since they can abide by an anti-Christian morality, which includes in its ethical code the modernised values of strength and independence (the rest of us are sheep). The fabled Nietzschean *Übermensch* (Superman) will invoke their 'will to power' to create new meanings and impose a new order to modernity. This order valorises the supreme role of human freedom in the world, replacing monotheism, while defeating nihilism.

Just like their inspiration, Heidegger, the moderates see Nietzsche's anthropocentric response to nihilism as dangerous.

The view that there's nothing more important than human freedom has various negative consequences, especially when coupled with 'scientism', the modern cultural attitude that prizes the ability to objectify, control, and instrumentalise the world to gratify our ever-increasing desires. One bad consequence of this combination is that it restricts and impoverishes our access to other sources of existential meaning. The radically free man, the new surrogate for God, treats everything as instrumental to his will: religion, family, and community are important only insofar as relations with them have utility and benefit. Once they cease being useful or become uninteresting, they are easy to discard, like broken toys or spoiled wine or junk email. Our shared world, in short, is rendered trivial and fungible to a man-god who puts his quest for self-determination above all else. Worse, other people with their own wills to power become competition, so we are left with a Nietzschean dystopia populated by neurotic, power-hungry, but ultimately isolated and embittered individuals.

Another terrible consequence of being free and Machiavellian about human relations is that you become entirely responsible for your own failure. If you flunk at becoming the next Elon Musk or Jeff Bezos, then you can't be in the *Übermensch* squad: you truly are ordinary and boring, not having achieved anything of value or global recognition. The moderates then link the burden to be great and extraordinary to our anxieties about modern life: to escape this burden, we look for distractions (video games, Netflix, #instalife); to approximate greatness, we crave for temporary highs (drugs, extreme sports, #YOLO); to rebel against the burden to be exceptional, we dissociate and become lonely, bored, or angry outsiders. How Thomas Hobbes famously described man outside human society now rings true inside an anthropocentric culture, they think: here, man's life is solitary, poor, nasty, brutish, and .... Hobbes' last word was 'short', but since we all tend to live much longer now, thanks to modern medicine, 'long' (but boring). It's hard not to see this kind of life as unfulfilling, according to the moderates, even absurd. And so, despair and alienation come knocking...

So if man is nihilism's instigator (for killing God), champion (for turning himself into a demi-god), and victim (for suffering its bad consequences), then it seems unlikely that we can save ourselves from ourselves. According to Taylor, Dreyfus, and Kelly, liberation from the bad outcome of modern nihilism requires the participation of something other than the human: something mysterious, more powerful, and definitely not so mortal and worldly. They call it the *sacred*.

So what is the sacred? They think of it as a non-human power traditionally articulated through religion. It goes by many forms and descriptions (magical, mystical, supernatural, holy) and is attributed to different dimensions of reality (transcendent, or otherworldly; immanent, or within the world). While a broad concept, there are similar features to the sacred across cultures and generations. Coming into contact or possession of something sacred, or performing rituals that are considered sacred, can have various phenomenological (felt) effects. If you're religious, think of the comfort and protection you get from praying the rosary or burning bukhoor incense. If New Age spirituality is your thing, think of the sensation of being grounded in the present moment after chanting OM post-yoga, or while brooding over gemstones and crystals. If sport is a big part of your life, think of finding yourself emboldened by wearing a red shirt before a gruelling game. These experiences can be said to fall into the non-rational, pre-modern, and anti-scientific way of approaching the world.[2] After all, why should the colour of your jersey have any bearing on your chances of winning, or the roundness of fruits on the dinner table have any say about the fate of our lot next year? While some sound kookier than others, the copiousness of these lucky charms and mundane superstitions suggests to the moderates that there's more going on beneath the surface of these cultural practices. They remind us that we're part of a larger, albeit mysterious world, one full of meaning and purpose we can't fully decipher. (Exactly the sense of mystery that the opponents of Enlightenment thought was threatened by nihilism, as we saw in the history chapter). These sacred experiences leave us with existential wonder and a deep sense of connection with life, its history, and our respective traditions and communities, as the moderates see it, and that's why they're hard to let go.

The sacred is also supposed to illuminate and draw out the best in us. Taylor talks about the concept of the moral source, or a concept that 'the contemplation, respect, or love of which enables us to get closer to what is good', empowering us to 'live up to what is higher' and aim for ends that are 'valuable, worthy, admirable'.[3] He mentions Plato's Idea of the pure, unadulterated Good that exists beyond the world of the senses, the Judeo-Christian God, and the Kantian notions of agency and human dignity as moral sources. These ideas aid us in becoming better people: they help us to examine the principles of a good life, to love our neighbours as we love ourselves, and to respect the inviolable rights of others and commit to our ethical duties. Expressions of these ideas – religious treatises, the figure of the cross, a copy of Kant's *Groundwork of the Metaphysics of Morals* – are not sacred in a material sense, of course. But they are in relation to the moral sources they symbolise and illuminate. Becoming animated by the sacred can deeply transform who we are and the way the world looks to us. Or at least, that's the thought.

The moderates think that a *renewed* articulation of the sacred might save us from the scourge of emptiness and despair which they think nihilism produces, since encounters with the sacred are sources of existential and spiritual enrichment. Heidegger warned how the culture of scientism, and of our obsession with manipulating reality, can obstruct the way the world might relate to human beings, and this is the concern driving the moderates. Adopting a scientistic way of life, according to Heidegger, stifles our ability to listen to the voice of Being and kills off possibilities of wonder. He also thinks that art can redeem us from the ills of scientism, since it can reveal the people, things, and events that most deserve attention, care, and participation in each culture. He cites Vincent Van Gogh's *A Pair of Shoes*, C. F. Meyer's poem 'The Roman Fountain' (1882), and a Greek temple at Paestum as the kind of artwork that illuminates 'life-worlds', serving as our sacred exemplars for focusing and preserving our human practices. Heidegger thinks that the sacred takes on many forms and expressions throughout history, and that there are certain *exceptional* people – the chosen prophets of Being: artists, poets, novelists, and philosophers like himself, naturally – with the skill to convey the sacred in our modern culture.

The American philosophers Dreyfus and Kelly feel this same Heideggerian itch for the spiritual. To animate our relationship with the sacred, they propose a modernised polytheism. In their view, the sacred is alive and thriving but goes unrecognised as such today. But if we *really* pay attention, we discover the sacred constantly manifesting itself in various recognisable phenomena: in 'whooshing up' with fellow fans in a Premier League final, being in the flow of expert sushi-making, or witnessing majestic Roger Federer tennis (that novelist David Foster Wallace once dubbed as a religious experience served on a television screen).[4] During these moments, 'something so overpowering happens that it wells up before you as a palpable presence and carries you along as on a powerful wave'.[5] If we are to have fulfilling lives, we need to be receptive to the sacred and to participate when it is at play.

Dreyfus and Kelly examine the way of life illustrated in Homerian epics for inspiration. In the *Odyssey* (8th B.C.), the best kinds of people – the heroes, the adventurers, even the face that launched a thousand ships – were attuned to Olympian divinities, which represented the highest Ancient Greek ideals. They suggest that receptivity to the call of their gods, who guided the 'moods' of different life situations, allowed human beings to *shine*:

> What makes Helen great in Homer's world is her ability to live a life that is constantly responsive to golden Aphrodite, the shining example of the sacred erotic dimension of existence. Likewise, Achilles had a special kind of receptivity to Ares and his warlike way of life; Odysseus had Athena, with her wisdom and cultural adaptability, to look out for him. Presumably, the master craftsmen of Homer's world worked in the light of Hephaestus's shining.[6]

Living meaningfully was about resonating with various forms of human excellence. Unfortunately, myths and old gods don't have a clear-cut role to play in our modern world. We'll find it impossible to hit it off with Anansi- or Freya-types at this stage, not with all our knowledge and technological savviness and smug modern scepticism. Our task is to figure out what will bring out our excellence as *modern* humans, in light of what the existentially meaningful 'moods' of our history and culture are. Together with Heidegger's reminder that art can save us, Dreyfus and Kelly think that there is much to learn from our history: 'Homer's wonder and Aeschylus' caring mood of cultivation, Dante's bliss, Luther's joy, and Descartes' calm mood of quiet reflection'.[7] Through these moods, we can become inspired to act and live meaningfully. We can cultivate the skill of deciphering various forms of the sacred and learn how to respond appropriately. The point behind modern polytheism is that, contra anthropocentrism, intensity and meaning *cannot* be imposed on experience (and we nihilists agree: you can't *build* a meaning of life). But the moderates think that the kind of intense meaning they think the meaning of life used to give us can still become part of the human experience, when individuals are in sync with the sacred that energises modern life. In short, polytheism is one way of buffering the effects of modern nihilism, since it is 'a saving possibility after the death of God: it would allow us to survive the breakdown of monotheism while resisting the descent into a nihilistic existence'.[8] Make no mistake, this existential argument about nihilism and the polytheistic sacred has a lot of appeal: in 2006, Dreyfus's course on 'Man, God, and Society in Western

Literature – From Gods to God and Back' was ranked the 58th most popular webcast on Apple iTunes, garnering Dreyfus a cult following online.[9]

Taylor doesn't go as far as advocating polytheism, but his theory of expressivism makes a similar point: a 'heightened, more vibrant quality of life' is accessible through meaningful encounters with art.[10] But not just any kind of art; the art needs to be *epiphanic*, in the sense of it having the power to disclose authentic claims made on us by the world. The world speaks, and geniuses can hear and decipher what it says without being tainted by anthropocentrism. In Taylor's view, great poets, painters, and novelists have articulated meaningful, non-random, and non-subjective reality in modernity. But more than translating these messages from the world, Taylor thinks that the epiphanic revelations of artists and writers can help us find our inner link with a larger order, or map out our place as human beings in the universe. Sound familiar? Taylor's approach seems to broach a return to the cosmological hierarchies of religion; and the appeal to artistic sensibility is the very same one which originally gave us the term 'the meaning of life'. Unlike Dreyfus and Kelly, who are sceptical of monotheism, Taylor thinks that we must be open to rekindling our relationship with God. He never really gets into the details of what this renewed theism is all about, but he seems convinced that it's a great way of shielding us from the threat of meaninglessness and melancholia. After all, what is genuinely sacred can only be transcendent, and what is ultimately transcendent can only be the highest being in the chain. And so, we loop back to the God-problem.

To sum up: Taylor, Dreyfus, and Kelly share the idea that to overcome nihilism – a nihilism caused by our anthropocentrism, a problem for which we are to blame – we need to revamp our relationship with sacred sources of meaning. Human beings need the sacred to help curb that part of us which seems intent on destroying itself, they think. What is crucial, what saves us from this man-made nihilism, is the *non-human* quality of the sacred. We need guidance, and if we look hard, we can find it.

But we argue that the strategy of modernising the sacred contra nihilism is a step backwards, for three reasons. First, the idea behind overcoming nihilism panders to a misplaced fear of it. Nihilism has had a bad theoretical and historical rap. The initial opposition to it was opposition to reason itself, to trying to understand our situation and using that understanding to improve it. Then as reason marched on, with the science and technology that made major improvements to life (clean water, effective medicine, more fun), nihilism became associated with 'levelling', a grinding down to the level of the 'herd'. It also became associated with pessimism, because some saw the demise of the meaning of life as a cue to make a dodgy evaluation of whether life's worth living, or whether collective suicide might be a better idea. Amid all the panic, snobbery, prejudice, and bad reasoning we've witnessed, it's best to remember the Russian women who marched under the banner of 'nihilism' in the hope of being allowed to study at university. The old world of mystery, where the lives of peasants and aristocrats flowed in accordance with the mysterious meaning they could sense, probably isn't something we should model our future on, even if there was any chance of reclaiming its rosy essence, if indeed it had one.

Second, the strategy cages us inside the 'overcoming' framework that both religious believers and atheists could benefit from escaping. Within that cage, the problem of meaninglessness is a constant danger we need to struggle against, a premise we can't question. This position blinds us from seeing the possibility that nihilism is something that our culture can take for granted as the natural stance for atheists, and a tolerable and understandable belief for the religious (we think that it can be!). Third, the strategy misidentifies the real issue.

Taylor, Dreyfus, and Kelly are responding to problems they perceive in modern life, and which they attribute to nihilism. They also identify the source as anthropocentrism. But if that's the case, then why not focus on correcting the cause so that we can prevent the effects? There is an answer that reframes the concerns of these moderates, inspired by the American pragmatist philosopher, Richard Rorty, who has candidly suggested that we can 'tell Zarathustra that the news that God is dead is not all that big a deal'. In this vein, we will argue that we need to outgrow the idea that nihilism is a problem to overcome.[11]

Rorty, we should warn you, appears unlikely to advance a philosophical conversation about modernity and the sacred. It's strange to even bring him up. As a pragmatist, a philosopher whose frame of reference is social utility, he is resolutely anti-metaphysical and eschews talk of the transcendent. He's mostly suspicious of religion and has poked fun at its more outrageous claims.[12] While he's been pejoratively called a nihilist by his critics (there are many), he neither characterises himself as one nor talks about nihilism in his work. But a closer look at his work shows that it can change the terms of the ongoing conversation on nihilism and the sacred. Instead of focusing on modern existential anxieties directly, Rorty is more concerned with egotism, or the intellectual, moral, and spiritual rigidity of people in terms of thinking and behaviour. He suspects that egotism is an expression of the satiating comfort behind the promise of certainty, both tendered by the cultures of religion, science, and more specifically, the philosophical interpretation of them as closed systems of knowledge – final answers about which there is nothing more to be said. Our dependence on these systems, which derive their authority from the universal and the non-human, prevents us from fully embracing a humanistic world according to Rorty. His work on self-creation and solidarity can be mobilised as ideals to fight against the culture of egotism. Rorty's approach, as we see it, allows us to outgrow the idea that nihilism is a problem, while addressing the concerns of the moderates more effectively.

What is egotism? Think of a holier-than-thou neighbour, who insists that all non-Christians will go to hell, or a chauvinist uncle who thinks that women are naturally weak, or that really obnoxious 'facts' guy from work who views religion as complete BS. They are probably egotists. They are self-centred not so much in being selfish, but in being self-satisfied with who they are and what they believe in. Egotists tend to have similar traits. They are dogmatic about their beliefs. They don't know how to listen. They may get electrified by debate, even enjoy riling up other people, but they never change their minds. They're stubborn and unlikeable except to their peers. They are condescending to those who aren't like them, since they think of themselves as redeemed from ignorance and consider the rest of us unenlightened. As a character flaw, mild forms of egotism are likely to be recognisable in people you know, from privileged homophobic parents to racist landlords. It is found in everyday life, and its normality is precisely what concerns Rorty.

Rorty isn't the first to complain about ordinary human vices like egotism, of course. The political theorist Judith Shklar thinks that most of our everyday relations are marked by cruelty, and that liberal politics should treat it as its central concern. The philosopher Hannah Arendt pointed out the dangers of banal evil: unimaginable destruction can be borne from lack of imagination, failure of empathy, and simple ambition (think of the Nazi war criminal Adolf Eichmann, who aloofly claimed that he was just following orders from his boss). Egotism is like cruelty and banal evil, but it's so mundane that we treat it more as annoying behaviour than a serious moral fault. Sure, nasty egotists can be good to their mothers and dogs. But their disinterest and refusal to understand what it's like to be other people, to listen to other views with respect, and to cooperate with projects whose aims don't fit into their rigid belief systems make them undesirable and potentially dangerous people.

But what causes egotism? It is closed-mindedness, that is, not being open to new ideas, conversation, and the possibility of being persuaded. Rorty had many ideas for what was at the root of this, and often looks like a philosopher who blames philosophy itself, but nevertheless closed-mindedness seems to be what most concerned him. Someone whose mind has been closed, because they think that they already know the truth and aren't prepared to question their beliefs, has a system of knowledge. Not a rational one they're ready to adjust in response to considerations they hadn't thought of before, but rather one that purports to be universal, fixed, and essential – that outlines, for the egotist, the final word about how things really are; in other words, the system functions as a grand design or a blueprint to the life of an egotist. You might say that it's their take on the meaning of life, one which they're not prepared to adjust. Their faith in this closed system gives egotists the confidence to make all sorts of dogmatic claims and issue moral judgements with bravado. No wonder Rorty thinks that many religious believers and philosophers are susceptible to egotism, since they obsess about being right all the time:

> They would like to go straight to the way things are (to the will of God, or the moral law, or the nature of human beings) without passing through other people's self-descriptions. Religion and philosophy have often served as shields for fanaticism and intolerance because they suggest that this sort of short-circuiting has been accomplished.[13]

Rorty, in short, militates against egotists who would rather be redeemed from impiety (if religious) or irrationality (if philosophical or scientific), instead of their intolerance, insensitivity, and their tendency to hurt other people. For him, egotism is a culturally entrenched disposition that we need to find a remedy for.

Rorty's strategy against egotism invokes the self against itself, an idea that is expressed well by the term 'self-enlargement'. There are two ways to self-enlarge, he thinks: self-creation and solidarity. Self-creation is best achieved when one *loses* the self to *create* the self. You self-create by expanding your repertoire of human experiences and encountering a great variety of human beings, since 'being authentic, being faithful to ourselves, is being faithful to something which was produced in collaboration with a lot of other people'.[14] A self-creator, in Rorty's terms, is deeply interested in other cultures. She watches movies and theatre, reads a lot of books, travels to different places, and learns from the experiences of other people. She knows that the more imaginative resources she has, the greater her chances of being able to weave an idiosyncratic life narrative. In short, the self-creator is the opposite of the egotist, whose life is self-enclosed rather than ever-growing. Solidarity, meanwhile, is the loyalty shared by a community of individuals with common beliefs, desires, and moral concerns. The existence of different loyalties is often a source of conflict. In Rorty's view, our task is to expand our conception of loyalty. The solidarity that does this kind of loyalty-expanding work is democratic solidarity, with its highest goal being to promote freer, happier, and richer lives for everyone in society. The more we consider other people as part of our kin, the better we recognise and respect their rights to pursue their versions of happiness and projects of self-creation. Consequently, since we see them as part of our moral circle, we are also inspired to make sure that our social and political institutions protect the rights and interests of all, and not just the few. Oscar Wilde's dictum 'socialism for the sake of individualism' is a nice way of summing up the point (the point being that we become freer because of other people – it's hard to be yourself when you live in such an unequal society that you're in constant danger of crime, for instance).

Self-creation and solidarity combat egotism by focusing our moral energy towards becoming more other-orientated, to opening our minds to what others have to say and attaining more sensitivity to reason. They divert our attention from ourselves to others. And the relevance of combating egotism to the problem which the moderates see in nihilism, is that when egotists invest everything in their own Nietzschean will to power, backed up by their closed system of belief, then when things go wrong – when they fail to become the next Elon Musk or Jeff Bezos, or they meet someone with a better grasp of their own system of knowledge, be it science or scripture – then they lose the claim to privilege and become susceptible to existential angst, powerlessness, and disillusionment. In this reading, egotism produces the symptoms which the moderates misdiagnose as resulting from nihilism.

The formula is pretty simple: address the cause (egotism) to nullify or prevent the bad effects from taking place (existential despair). Taylor, Dreyfus, and Kelly recognise that the negative phenomena which concern them are produced by anthropocentrism gone haywire, but it is really only a certain kind of anthropocentrism, namely closed-minded egotism rooted in the complete self-assuredness that Nietzsche thought the Supermen would use to overcome nihilism and make the world meaningful again. As such, the real problem is not being addressed in the moderates' accounts, and once again, poor old nihilism gets the blame. Taylor focuses on non-human moral sources and a modernised understanding of the transcendent. Dreyfus and Kelly argue that we have an entire array of contemporary spiritual forces to lean on for existential meaning. All three want to 're-enchant' the modern world. Rorty changes the terms of this discussion in a very useful way, because unlike Taylor, Dreyfus, and Kelly, his project tries to nip the problem in the bud by rearing the horns of egotism against itself, giving us a moral-existential solution to a moral-existential problem. Nihilism is not a moral-existential proposition; if it's true, it's a fact about reality. Overall, then, Rorty remains true to the Enlightenment motto of liberating ourselves from our self-incurred immaturity, by sidestepping what seems to be a return to non-human worship in the writings of the moderates.

If we attend to egotism, we have a chance of warding off disillusionment, disengagement, and anxiety. If self-enlargement were fostered as a moral ideal, we could address the problems of egotism, and the latent negative effects lying in its wake with a single blow. Naturally, Rorty's methods of self-creation and solidarity are up for critical debate, but his strategy is clearly a step forward, since it unhinges the 'overcoming nihilism' framework that has held sway for far too long now. Rorty is shooting at the right target, and it makes sense to follow suit. Egotism is a problem, nihilism isn't.

Notes

1 Nietzsche, *The Gay Science*, 181.
2 A popular anecdote: a visitor noticed a horseshoe hanging above the entrance of the home of Nobel Prize-winning physicist Niels Bohr. The visitor asked if Bohr believed that horseshoes brought good luck. Bohr replied: 'No, but I am told that they bring luck even to those who do not believe in them'.
3 Taylor, *Sources of the Self*, 92–6.
4 Wallace, 'Roger Federer as Religious Experience'.
5 Dreyfus and Kelly, *All Things Shining*, 194.
6 Dreyfus and Kelly, *All Things Shining*, 62.
7 Dreyfus and Kelly, 'Saving the Sacred from the Axial Revolution', 202.
8 Dreyfus and Kelly, *All Things Shining*, 61.
9 Quinn, 'The iPod Lecture Circuit'.

10 Taylor, *Sources of the Self*, 373.
11 Rorty, 'Reply to J.B. Schneewind', 507.
12 Rigsbee recalls a story from Rorty: one day, Rorty found himself on a panel with the Dalai Lama. Rorty said that he had to suppress the urge to ask His Holiness to levitate ('Rorty from a Poet's View', 143).
13 Rorty, 'Redemption from Egotism', 395.
14 Rorty, 'In a Flattened World', 3.

Bibliography

Dreyfus, Hubert and Sean Dorrance Kelly. *All Things Shining: Reading the Western Classics to Find Meaning in a Secular Age*. New York: Free Press, 2011.

Dreyfus, Hubert and Sean Dorrance Kelly. 'Saving the Sacred from the Axial Revolution'. *Inquiry: An Interdisciplinary Journal of Philosophy* 54, no. 2 (2011): 195–203.

Nietzsche, Friedrich. *The Gay Science*. Translated by Walter Kaufmann. New York: Random House, 1974.

Quinn, Michelle. 'The iPod Lecture Circuit'. *The Los Angeles Times*, November 24, 2007. Archived by Wayback Machine. https://web.archive.org/web/20160304052136/, http://socrates.berkeley.edu/~hdreyfus/pdf/Los%20Angeles%20Times_%20The%20iPod%20lecture%20circuit.pdf

Rigsbee, David. 'Rorty from a Poet's View'. *New Literary History* 3, no. 1 (2008): 141–3.

Rorty, Richard. 'In a Flattened World, Review of *The Ethics of Authenticity* 1991 by Charles Taylor'. *The London Review of Books*, April 9, 1993. https://www.lrb.co.uk/the-paper/v15/n07/richard-rorty/in-a-flattened-world

Rorty, Richard. 'Redemption from Egotism: James and Proust as Spiritual Exercises'. In *The Rorty Reader*. Edited by Christopher Voparil and Richard J. Bernstein, 389–406. New Jersey: Wiley-Blackwell, 2010.

Rorty, Richard. 'Reply to J.B. Schneewind'. In *The Philosophy of Richard Rorty*. Edited by Randall Auxier and Lewis Edwin Hahn, 506–8. Chicago, IL: Open Court, 2010.

Taylor, Charles. *Sources of the Self: The Making of Modern Identity*. Cambridge, MA: Harvard University Press, 1992.

Wallace, David Foster. 'Roger Federer as Religious Experience'. *The New York Times,* August 20, 2006. https://www.nytimes.com/2006/08/20/sports/playmagazine/20federer.html

5 Revaluating Nihilism

The term 'nihilism' is an infamous trigger of negative responses. Its use attracts attention, and in our neo-liberal techno-world of instant likes and insults, all publicity is good publicity, right? There are two opposite ends to the contemporary spectrum of fascination with nihilism. On the one end are the philosophical moralists, religious or otherwise, who use it as a buzzword to bring to mind things that worry them and which they really don't like – usually without telling us what those things are, exactly. Accusing someone of being a nihilist is the worst insult of the True Moralist, a verdict of condemnation against interlocutors they find guilty of a range of faults. These faults tend to circle around outrage at anyone having the gall to deny there is a meaning of life: 'you have no values, you can't be trusted, you blithely accept that you have nothing to live for .... you *nihilist*!' If the 'nihilist' doesn't agree, and responds, 'sure I've got values and I've got plenty to live for too', then they must be trivial, shallow, hollow, a symptom of the degrading nihilistic techno-capitalist culture we've adopted, where nothing really matters anymore. In debates about ethics and morality set up by these True Moralists, the charge of nihilism frequently works as a conversation-stopper, one designed to draw the line between the philosophical and the personal – they hurl it to cast doubt on their opponents' character and personal integrity.

On the other end of the spectrum are the pessimists and haters, who embrace doom and despair with gusto: 'everything is terrible, didn't you know? Well I'm going to spell it out for you (with glee!) because I'm someone who looks reality in the eye and never flinches'. It's hard not to suspect that the unbearable gloom of cosmically pessimistic philosophers has something to do with the curious perception that negativity is profound and cool: 'stop deluding yourselves, the world is a dung heap, be a *dangerous* thinker, like me!' The titles of some of the popular nihilism titles on the market today say it all; we're not going to mention them by name because we're not going to discuss them (although we did suffer reading some), but you can find the kind of title we're talking about in seconds. They show a morbid fascination with the claims that God is dead, life is meaningless, morality is a sham, and human beings have no intrinsic purpose. They use these ideas to provide apparent depth to their attempts to portray human life in the most appalling light possible: here's a terrible example of human suffering; here's a terrible example of human cruelty; here's something Schopenhauer said: didn't you know that you're almost certainly going to fail in life then die horribly, alone and in pain? Despite being around for ages, the philosophy inserted into these one-sided narratives still sounds scandalous to folks without a formal academic background in philosophy. Most importantly, the combined package is all very provocative, so it sells.

The moral brigade wants to keep an aura of fear around their chosen enemy, nihilism, and if it stays vague, that's a good thing, because it makes it easier for their critiques to hit the mark (you can't miss if nobody knows where the bullseye is). Many people have the feeling that there's something wrong with our current society. But if you think about it, people have *always* thought that about their own current society, whenever and wherever that was, and they've always been right – so it's easy to be persuaded that the deep cause is something called 'nihilism'; if nihilism is a historical process, then that'll explain the deterioration they've been witnessing. Meanwhile, the sinister brigade reaps the practical rewards of their all-consuming pessimism in the form of cult followings and book contracts, T-shirts with Nietzsche slogans, lines from their writings incorporated into TV shows and rap songs, that kind of thing. Both camps have a strong vested interest in maintaining the bad reputation of nihilism. Without the dark side of the force for the Jedi to resist and the Sith to embrace, there wouldn't be any *Star Wars*.

We recognise that 'nihilism' has become a repository of multifarious and confusing meanings; we haven't tried to hide that. But we've argued that there is a clear and robust definition of nihilism we can work with, one conceptually grounded in the history of Western philosophy, which is still the core idea no author can entirely get away from, no matter how hard they try: nihilism is the view that there is no meaning of life. This view arose in relation to the historical threat of atheism in the 18th century and alongside the theme of the meaning of life (its twin), which are intellectual concerns themselves shaped by European politics, religious, social, and economic contingencies, as well as various philosophical temperaments. If we uncouple nihilism from concerns that have arisen about the consequences of people thinking that life is meaningless, concerns which believers and atheists have shared, then we can learn to see 'nihilism' in a new light: as a useful and straightforward label for a useful and credible philosophical view. Nobody's required to use the word our way, of course. But if you're going to suppose that 'nihilism' is terrible, disconcerting, shocking, or otherwise problematic, then please begin by telling us what you mean by the word. Once you've done that, feel free to devise your action plan for escaping from nihilism, draw out the terrible consequences we're stuck with, or whatever – but tell us what you mean first. It's not much to ask.

We might be getting greedy now, but there's one more thing we'd ask in addition to clarity, namely a little historical sensitivity. In recent years, some moral philosophers have defined 'nihilism' as 'nothing is right or wrong, or morally good or bad'.[1] That ticks the clarity box. But the problem with this particular definition is that it takes its lead from a historical association which is confused, or at the very least, highly controversial. Why would *that* word seem appropriate for *that* idea, namely a complete lack of moral compass? Probably because Nietzsche toyed with the idea that without a meaning of life, there could be no truth about what's right or wrong, and perhaps no truth at all: 'Is there still any up or down?' after the 'death of God', he asked, 'Are we not straying, as through an infinite nothing?'[2] Even more famously, Dostoevsky linked these ideas about ethics and morality in his novel *The Brothers Karamazov* (1880): '"But what will become of men then?" I asked him, "without God and immortal life?" All things are lawful then, they can do what they like?'[3] This historical association is the reason 'nihilism' has seemed like a good word for the view that nothing is morally right or wrong. But we've argued that the absence of a meaning of life doesn't give us a reason to believe nothing can be morally good or bad. The association of the word 'nihilism' with that kind of dubious (and probably unliveable) immoralism results from historical worries that have never been substantiated, and which the contemporary authors who use it this way surely wouldn't accept. And anyway, there's already a perfectly good word for not believing that there's any right or wrong, one that drives the point home without any unnecessary conceptual confusion: 'immoralism'. There's no other word for the view that there's no meaning of life – only 'nihilism' fits the bill.

Just like nihilism's association with immoralism, its association with pessimism is born from the disappointed dream of onto-theology ('onto', from the Greek for being or existence). Onto-theology, at its core, measures the quality of every human life against cosmic meanings and non-human standards built into the nature of reality. Naturally, the higher the flight, the harder the fall, so when life fell short of these standards with the advent of atheism, a new, secular evaluation of human life seemed like a good idea. Beginning in onto-theological disappointment, however, it's no surprise that the calculative cost-benefit appraisal of life which resulted was to end in pessimism. Trying to judge human life is a secular attempt at being God-like, and applied to life in general, the judgement is best left to God in his omniscience; God might know enough to make the judgement, but not a human being. And applied to individual lives, the task can be rephrased into something like this: 'let's weigh your entire existential worth, shall we?' We don't know about you, but we think human lives don't deserve to be reduced to an equation or a checklist.

Consider old Uncle Bob – he married, had a couple of kids, did his job OK, and these days he mainly enjoys going to the pub, watching the telly, and betting on the horses. Too many contemporary philosophers love this kind of example – if you read that stuff, you'll know how hackneyed it has become.[4] That's because it illustrates, for them, the idea of a life that isn't very meaningful, in preparation for their analysis of what a truly meaningful life consists in. Psychologists get involved too, devising scientific criteria for living a meaningful life. But all this strikes us as quite condescending to poor old Uncle Bob, who's always going to get a terrible score.

Bob's life didn't have any great social significance. He'd admit that himself. Do we have to rephrase it, by means of some onto-theological terminology from 18th-century German philosophy, into a condemnation? Can't we just say that his life had no great social significance? (This seems to be the feature of Bob's life that makes philosophers want to judge his life as not very meaningful.) Similarly, if people with problems in their lives have learned to say that they're worried their lives have become meaningless (or always were), as some have, and the aim is to help them, as it is for the psychologists, then can't we just focus on the particular problems? If they suffer from lack of motivation, we could just say: 'they suffer from lack of motivation'. Then, there's no more need to torture ourselves trying to find the correct analysis of a 'meaningful' life – with the ever-present background implication that if human life as a whole lacks cosmic meaning, as atheists are almost bound to think, then the whole human race is condemned. In this language game about meaning, atheists are trapped: they must evade, deny, regret, or at least shrug off and say they don't care – either way it's still something bad, just like if an individual is said to have a meaningless life. But all we need to do is drop the idea of 'meaningful' and 'meaningless' as evaluations of life, in accordance with nihilism. Then, there's no more need to judge Uncle Bob, and no more need to condemn the human race – not if *everyone* has a meaningful life at the individual level (Bob's meaning included bringing up kids and betting on horses, not winning the Nobel Peace Prize), and *nobody* has one at the collective level. Dubious evaluation has thereby been replaced by fact.

Think of it this way: if your life is meaningful for other people, it probably is for you too. Maybe some hermits have been exceptions, and maybe some people don't give a damn what others think, but as an almost universal rule, a person's sense that they're living a meaningful life depends on the meaning their lives have for other people, especially their loved ones. A nihilist needn't dispute the importance of this, and shouldn't, because if you start to feel that you're a waste of space, it can be a serious problem. What nihilism disputes is that this sense is a guide to how close you are to a feature of reality called 'the meaning of life'. The sense isn't rendered illusory because there's no meaning of life, since what it taps into could be any number of things, depending on what most concerns you. Being useful and loved is enough for most people to feel that their lives are meaningful in a good way, and this isn't illusory. Life itself is meaningless, but individual lives are meaningful in innumerable ways, and it is the ways the individual cares most about which sustains their sense of living meaningfully. It might be morally good if everyone cared about being morally good, but those who don't will never be told they're wrong by the nature of reality, only by other people.

You might think that our defence of nihilism is too sober, reasonable, and boring. How anti-climactic! Nietzsche and Heidegger made nihilism an existential threat, Schopenhauer and the pessimists made it a source of pathos, even the moderates, like Dreyfus, make it a big scary problem we need to deal with. Some might conclude that the lack of drama shows that we're true nihilists. And they'd be right, except that they'd probably say this as an accusation with an unspecified negative connotation; in this case, they'd be leaning on something to do with being shallow. But the concern driving our defence of nihilism throughout this book has been of serious intent and is as follows: we don't think the meaning of life is an idea that should be retained in the transition from a religious to an atheistic context. We think it does more harm than good. Nihilists don't think there is a meaning of life, and there's no better way to dispel an idea about something than to deny that the 'something' exists. Cultivating rational scepticism about the existence of witchcraft is what dealt the greatest blow to the pernicious usage of that idea, an idea which led to women being drowned and burned.

Many people with religious beliefs think there is a meaning of life, but few would claim to know what it is, exactly. Usually, the idea ends at living well, in accordance with the moral precepts of your religion, and in the hope of reward – the contribution this makes to the ultimate cosmic plan is left somewhat shrouded. We don't think this idea translates well into a non-religious context, where it will be almost impossible to keep it coupled to a moral context, and where people can devise very specific plans for how to perfect the human race, thereby eradicating meaningless existence. Unless the meaning of life idea is explicitly renounced by embracing nihilism, then it will linger on in harmful ways; it is too pervasive and unreflected to simply be ignored. And that self-conscious renouncement can never happen while 'nihilism' remains in the hands of extremists and alarmists. Until nihilism is rehabilitated, people without religious conviction will carry on believing in the meaning of life, however unreflectively, and a barrier will exist to realising the following:

1 Reality does not require us to judge or evaluate human life as a whole. We are not accountable to a cosmic standard or existential barometer, only to each other – because there's no meaning of life.
2 Reality does not require us to judge or evaluate individual lives according to their meaning. Lives can only have different meanings to different people – because there's no meaning of life.
3 There's no guarantee that everything's going to turn out fine for the human race and there's never going to be an endgame which makes it all worthwhile in the end. If we want a prosperous future, we'll have to work on it (unless we're very lucky), and different people will have different ideas about what we should do. Watch out for egotists pushing their take on the meaning of life. There's everything to play for – because there's no meaning of life.

4   There's no guarantee that everything's going to turn out fine in the end for you personally and there's no endgame to make it all worthwhile; you just die, and if scientists work out how to make you live forever, there still won't be an endgame. If you want a prosperous future, and for others to think your life is worthwhile, then you'll have to work on it (unless you're very lucky). Watch out for egotists trying to make their own lives meaningful. There's everything to play for – because there's no meaning of life.

There are many kinds and levels of meanings, from the trivial and the functional (brushing teeth, learning how to drive) to the identity-defining and life-shaping (divorce, death of a loved one). But they derive their importance and worth from the choices we make, the community we are part of, and the world we have built, and not in relation to a divine plan or a glorious destiny pushed by an egotist. In the same way that we treat the secular turn as a historical event – something that required time, rational deliberation, and the right circumstances in place for it to come alive in the world (in Kantian terms, the right 'conditions of possibility') – unlearning our misconceptions about nihilism should be approached that way too. It is something that *happens*. It requires deliberation. It is something we need to work on.

Deliberation often starts in an act of imagination – a 'what if'. What if nihilism wasn't so bad? What if it were a useful tool in an overly judgemental world? What if it helped us to focus on particular problems? What if it helped us to imagine a better future? What if it's true? If it was, what would you do differently?

Notes

1 Dreier, 'Moral Relativism and Moral Nihilism', 240.
2 Nietzsche, *The Gay Science,* 181–2.
3 Dostoyevsky, *The Brothers Karamazov,* 762.
4 The two most influential philosophical analyses of what makes an individual person's life meaningful (as opposed to the human race), the ones that have since inspired a massive literature, were made by Susan Wolf (2008; first published in 1997) and, in much more detail, Thaddeus Metz (2013).

Bibliography

Dreier, James. 'Moral Relativism and Moral Nihilism'. *The Oxford Handbook of Ethical Theory*, 240–64. Edited by David Copp. Oxford: Oxford University Press, 2006.

Dostoyevsky, Fyodor. *The Brothers Karamazov.* Translated by Constance Garnett. New York: The Lowell Press, 2019. https://www.gutenberg.org/files/28054/28054-pdf.pdf

Metz, Thaddeus. *Meaning in Life.* Oxford: Oxford University Press, 2013.

Nietzsche, Friedrich. *The Gay Science.* Translated by Walter Kaufmann. New York: Random House, 1974.

Wolf, Susan. 'Meaning in Life'. In *The Meaning of Life: A Reader,* 232–5. Edited by E.D. Klemke and Steven Kahn. Oxford: Oxford University Press, 2008.

Index

Aeschylus 45
Arendt, H. 47
Augustine, Saint 7, 13

Beiser, F. 32
Benatar, D. 31, 34–5
Berlin, I. 18
Bezos, J. 42, 50

Chaussard, P. J-B 17

Dante 45
Darwin, C. 34
Dawkins, R. 34
Descartes, R. 45
Dostoevsky, F. 55
Dreyfus, H. 39–47, 50–1, 57
Du Noyer, A-M P. 13–14

Epicurus 14

Federer, R. 44
Fichte, J.G. 18–21, 23, 30, 40

Galton, F. 34
Gertz, N. 1–2
Gillespie, M.A. 2
Götze, F.L. (Goetzius) 13–14

Hamann, J.G. 16
Hancock, H. 6
Hardy, T. 34
Hartmann, E. von 33–4
Heidegger, M. 23–4, 36, 39, 41, 44–5, 57
Hobbes, T. 13, 15, 42

Holbach 15–16, 18, 28
Homer 44–5
Horace 28

Jacobi, F.H. 15–20, 23–4, 28
Jenische, D. 17–18, 20
Jesus 13
Jünger, E. 2

Kant, I. 15, 17–20, 30, 41, 43–4, 59
Kelly, S. 39–47, 50–1
Kierkegaard, S. 21–4

Ledger, H. 2
Leopardi, G. 28–9
Lessing, G.E. 15–16
Lucretius 14
Luther, M. 45

Maistre, J. de 16
Mendelssohn, M. 15–17
Meyer, C.F. 44
Mitchell, E. 33
Musk, E. 42, 50

Nietzsche, F. 7–8, 22–4, 27, 29, 39–42, 50–1, 54–5, 57
Novalis 20

Obereit, J.H. 14–15, 17–18, 20

Plato 43

Rorty, R. 47–51
Rousseau, J-J 14, 18

Schlegel, F. 20
Schopenhauer, A. 4, 29–31, 33–5, 54, 57
Shakespeare, W. 2
Shklar, J. 48
Spinoza, B. 13, 16, 19

Taylor, C. 39–44, 46–7, 50–1
Theodorus the Atheist 15
Turgenev, I. 21–2

Unamuno, M. de 36

Van Goph, V. 44
Voltaire 14, 18

Wallace, D.F. 44
Wells, H.G. 1
Wilde, O. 50

Zorn, J. 33

For Product Safety Concerns and Information please contact our EU representative GPSR@taylorandfrancis.com
Taylor & Francis Verlag GmbH, Kaufingerstraße 24, 80331 München, Germany

www.ingramcontent.com/pod-product-compliance
Lightning Source LLC
Chambersburg PA
CBHW051104230426
43667CB00013B/2436